LOURDES:
CITY OF THE SICK

CATHERINE T. WATLING

LOURDES
City of the sick

ST PAULS

ST PAULS
Middlegreen, Slough SL3 6BT, United Kingdom
Moyglare Road, Maynooth, Co. Kildare, Ireland

© ST PAULS 1993

ISBN 085439 445 1

Produced in the EEC
Printed by The Guernsey Press Co, Guernsey, C.I.

ST PAULS is an activity of the priests and brothers of the Society
of St Paul who proclaim the Gospel through the media of social
communication

Contents

Author's acknowledgement

Thank you to the staff of the Information and Medical Bureaux in Lourdes for their assistance.

Thank you to all those kind people who sacrificed their leisure time during pilgrimages to lecture on the historical, architectural, religious and other aspects of Lourdes and thank you to the various authors whose books about Lourdes I have been reading avidly for many years.

A very special word of thanks to my loyal and helpful night nursing staff for their assistance and encouragement.

Publishers' acknowledgement

The publishers are grateful to the following for permission to reproduce the photos: Cover: E. Martino (© Periodici San Paolo); Pages 1 and 4 top: Catherine Watling; Pages 2 top, 3, 4 bottom, 5 top, 6 top: A. Giovannini (© Edizioni Paoline srl); Pages 6 bottom, 7 bottom: A. Tarzia (© Edizioni Paoline srl); Pages 5 bottom, 7 top: R. Risitano fsp.

Cover design: Mary Lou Winters fsp

Dedicated to the memory of Vincent and Canon E. McGough

Chapter 1
Con the shepherd

Con Brannigan was employed by one of the farmers in Fernlysthwaite, a small village in Cumbria. Con's days were spent in the company of his two border collies and the flocks of herdwick sheep on the wild and lonely Cumbrian fells.

He was 46 years old when I paid my first professional nursing visit to his humble home. His cottage was one of a group of four, located in a sort of no man's land, one mile from Fernlysthwaite and several miles from anywhere else faintly resembling civilization.

Con was a regular customer in the Woodside Inn, the lively little country pub situated in an elevated position. The lofty location provided a panoramic view of various stretches of Lakeland, studded with many remote hamlets and farmsteads. On a clear day, it allowed a distant vista of Morecambe Bay.

The Woodside Inn was a favourite drinking haunt for a variety of people, including my husband and myself. We regarded it as an ideal environment for relaxing and unwinding at weekends after a busy working week.

It was sited approximately one and a half miles from Fernlysthwaite, in the opposite direction to Con Brannigan's cottage. Every evening, without fail, the small, dark and wiry haired shepherd, with his weather-beaten face and quiet voice made the two and a half mile journey on foot. He was always accompanied by Ben, the larger of his two collies.

Ben, who relished his nightly drink of bitter beer, was accepted by staff and customers of the Woodside Inn as an important habitué. It was a well-known fact that Ben was often responsible for getting his master home safely.

Con's love of more than 'a wee drop of the hard stuff' frequently rendered him oblivious of his surroundings. His loyal canine companion, however, could always be relied upon to guide him through the dark deserted lanes, to the lowly cottage which was their home. Local people claimed that, often when they reached their destination, Mrs Brannigan refused them entry. On these occasions, man and dog walked back to Fernlysthwaite and bedded down for the night on the straw covered floor of the barn that belonged to Con's employer.

Due to the marked regularity of these nocturnal excursions, the few residents who constituted the small community in which the Brannigans lived, were accustomed to seeing the Irish man staggering all over the place. When Con developed an almost permanent, unsteady gait and several times fell flat on his face, there was a complete lack of sympathy from inside his home and outside of it.

His wife accused him of humiliating her and their two teenage sons. His employer joked with the shepherd, his quips suggesting that the little Irishman had a poteen still operating up yonder, in the fells. The big, good natured farmer would throw his head back and laugh loudly saying, "Ee Con, lad, go canny on that there moonshine, my auld son, or it will pop your clogs for you one of these days."

Unfortunately, it was not the alcoholic content in

the shepherd's blood stream, however high that concentration may have been, that was causing him to sway unsteadily and occasionally fall. It was the warning signal of multiple sclerosis.

Multiple sclerosis is one of the commonest neurological diseases. It is characterized by scattered patches of degeneration in the brain and spinal cord. It is a spasmodic ailment. Spasms may be separated by months or years. In the early stages, the attacks usually pass without any permanent disability. As the disease progresses, episodes frequently leave a remaining deficit. Outcome varies greatly.

Some patients suffering from multiple sclerosis may have little or no disability at the end of 20 years, while others may be severely paralyzed within three years. Sufferers are prone to chest and urinary infections. Sometimes there is evidence of euphoria or deprivation of intellectual ability. Usually, their speech is impaired. Steroid drugs, physiotherapy and encouragement to remain ambulant for as long as possible, were the only methods of treatment available 30 years ago.

It was a bitterly cold February morning in 1959 when I received a request from Doctor Wardle, one of our local general practitioners. He wished me to visit Mr Cornelius Brannigan, 2 Hillfoot Cottages, for the purpose of administering general nursing care. The cool, calm voice of the efficient surgery receptionist informed me that the provisional diagnosis, pending further investigations, was multiple sclerosis. Those two words stood out like a Belisha beacon from the diagnostic column of my work list book.

Although I did not know Mr Cornelius Brannigan personally, I was to a certain extent, acquainted with

11

Con, the shepherd. During the winter months, it had been his custom to bring his Herdwick flocks down from the windswept fells and tend to them in the more sheltered, low lying fields around Fernlysthwaite.

As I drove from my home in the market town of Helmsvale to patients who resided in the isolated surrounding areas, I frequently met the little wiry haired shepherd, his two border collies and his sheep straggling across the road. Normally he passed the time of day by stating it was 'a mucky auld mornin" or 'not a bad sort of a day for the time of the year'. His dulcet, Irish brogue prompted me to take our conversation a little further. I inquired as to what part of Ireland he hailed from.

Con replied, "Thurles, County Tipperary. But sure, Nurse, I've never been back next or near the place, since I left it when I was a broth of a lad at 18."

Patrons at the Woodside Inn were entertained on Friday and Saturday evenings by Dot, a pleasantly plump and rather garishly dressed, middle-aged pianist. Con, who always occupied a corner seat by the door, with his dog at his feet, never joined in the prevailing merriment. He spoke only when addressed by customers entering and leaving the premises. His seemingly limited vocabulary allowed merely 'Howdo' to those entering and 'Ta-ra' to those leaving.

No words were required when he wished to re-order, as the bar staff were so familiar with his drinking habits, that a slight movement of his forefinger produced a replenished glass almost immediately. Therefore, the general assumption of all concerned, was that the shepherd's presence in that corner was solely for the purpose of consuming as much liquor as he possibly could, in the allotted time.

He did not wish to waste precious drinking time in conversation or in singing. However, when I gave Dot my reason for requesting her to play 'It's a long way to Tipperary' and she acquiesced with a particularly boisterous rendering of the jaunty, marching air, only a little encouragement was needed to get the Irish man's feet tapping and his voice singing.

Ensuing Saturday nights when a few doubles of the hard stuff had loosened his tongue a little, his weather-beaten face would lighten. He would sing of his native country and how his heart lay right there.

As I drove through the peaceful village on that frosty February morning, bound for Hillfoot Cottages, my innermost feelings were a mixture of loneliness and sadness. I knew only too well that there was very little hope of seeing Con in his working capacity ever again.

The four grey stone built cottages stood on the right side of the narrow road, in an extremely unsheltered position. All around were stone built dykes separating the road from the fields. From behind the cottages, a stretch of grassland extended into the hills and the moorland beyond.

Chapter 2

Con's hospitalization

The tiny panes in the small window of Number Two were clean and sparkling, although the frame was almost devoid of paint. A large aspidistra in its green jardiniere filled the window space. The green curtains were arranged so they fell along each side of the leafy plant. This curtain-aspidistra arrangement prevented passers-by from obtaining a glimpse of the interior. The clumsy iron door knocker was in the form of a ram's head and the resounding noise which ensued when I used it, inevitably alerted the residents of the other three cottages, as well as the Brannigans.

Heavy footsteps approached the door from the inside. As the chains and bolts were being audibly removed, I heard a woman's voice announce, "Happen it's doctor or mebbe th'egg man." When the heavy door eventually creaked open, I found myself face to face with a tall, obese lady whose faded ginger hair was gathered tightly into an old-fashioned bun on the back of her head.

She wore a grey knitted skirt that reached the level of the fur trim of her down-at-heel, ankle boots. A matching dull grey jumper and cardigan completed her ensemble. Round her neck was a measuring tape and perched on the end of her pug nose was a pair of rimless spectacles.

I gazed in bewilderment at the quaint figure and

for a fleeting moment imagined that I had been cast back in time about 100 years. Mrs Brannigan spoke two words: "Through there." I followed the direction of her pointing thumb and that eerie sensation of being suddenly thrust into the Dickensian era engulfed me again.

The reasonably large kitchen-cum-living room had a stone-flagged floor which was scrubbed almost white. Three brightly multicoloured, hand woven peg rugs were doing their utmost to cover the greater part of the floor area. There was a black range with a brass rail above it and it seemed that the two were competing for brilliance.

An ancient dresser leaned against one wall. Hanging from its unsightly hooks was an assortment of cups, mugs and jugs. A variety of plates of different sizes, saucers, basins, a baking bowl and rolling pin were stacked on the surface of the dresser. A green curtain, similar to those on the window, draped the bottom part of this relic.

An equally archaic circular table with splayed, carved legs occupied the middle of the room. Its centre piece was a second aspidistra. Placed around the table were four high backed, cane bottomed chairs. Two rocking chairs, without upholstery and cushions stood like two old soldiers either side of the shining range. In a recess at the side of this unwieldy heating apparatus was Mrs Brannigan's source of income – a rather old-fashioned treadle sewing machine. This eccentric lady was the local dressmaker and seamstress. From her almost medieval machine, she produced bridal gowns and quite stylish outfits that the most modern fashion magazines would have been proud to display on their glossy pages.

Con Brannigan was lying in a most uncomfortable position on a camp bed by the window. The foot of the bed was almost level with the front door. He was getting the full force of the icy draught. I removed my coat. Mrs Brannigan sat down and resumed her treadling and stitching, ignoring me completely.

I looked at the pathetic little figure on the bed and said, "I thought you must be poorly, Con. I've missed seeing you round the lanes. How are you feeling?"

Some muttered words came from the direction of the sewing machine. Without stopping what she was so busily engaged in, Mrs Brannigan mimicked me by repeating word for word what I had just said. She went on to say, "He that loveth the danger shall perish therein. The evils of drink shall not go unnoticed by the Lord. Alcohol is nowt but the devil's brew but the Lord bides his own time. Oh aye, he does that."

When there was a lull in the sermon, I asked the industrious seamstress for a basin, soap, towel and some hot water. With her head lowered over the heavy tweed material in the machine and her fat feet moving forwards and backwards on the treadle, she jerked her thumb over her left shoulder.

She said, "Owt you need for him is in th'cupboard under t'dresser yonder. Water's in t'kettle on top of the range." I found what I needed with the exception of a towel and clean pyjamas. These articles I requested in the most courteous manner possible.

Mrs Brannigan rose from her chair. She removed her funny little spectacles, glowered at me, moved towards the range, opened the door of the warming oven, and flung a towel and a pair of red striped pyjamas straight at my face. Her action was immediately followed by a tirade of abuse. Almost screaming, she left me in no doubt whatsoever as to how she felt about her husband and his illness. Her vehement words poured forth,

"Now, look here, I'm not having nobody cum in to my own house and start ordering me about and most especially when that person is bothering over that no good drunk there. He's never troubled hissel about me or the lads. But for me them two boys would have hungered to death. I'm not having my place turned upside down and inside out every day of the week by you or anybody else." She poked a stubby forefinger at me, replaced her glasses on the end of her nose and resumed her stitching.

I kept very quiet. Firstly, because I was both startled and scared. Secondly, I did not wish to make the situation any worse than it already was for the helpless Con. The unnecessary harangue, however, following so quickly on the heels of the Bible citations, stirred within me a fervent desire to remove the weighty book from its moorings underneath the aspidistra plant on the cane table between the window and the camp bed and push it firmly into her face.

Instead, I turned towards Con and commenced the washing procedure that constituted general nursing care. There was no apparent contraction of any of his limbs, but his thin legs were powerless. Hoping that the whirring noise of the overworked machine would prevent his wife from overhearing, I said quietly into his left ear, "Tell me what happened, Con."

The large brown eyes set in the lean, weatherbeaten face looked at me as he answered, "Och sure, Nurse, I don't know at all, at all. It is as if the whole strength has been took out of my legs. Doctor Wardle thinks it's a chill I've caught and mebbe a wee bit of a stroke. Doctor thinks the strength will come back again. Do you think it will?"

Like the fun loving Doctor Wardle, I lied to Con as I cheerfully replied, "Oh yes, a lot of people suffer these slight strokes then get up and walk about as good as new. So don't worry, Doctor Wardle and I will work ever so hard on those legs of yours. Probably a little bit of exercise is all they need." No legs anywhere in the entire area had undergone more exercise in the past than the useless pair before me.

Mrs Brannigan, meanwhile, carried on a conversation with herself concerning "the devil's brew flowing in yon body". Once that happens, the good Lord most decidedly turns his back on the victim and hands him over to Satan forever. At one stage, she burst into song, "Oh God our help in ages past...".

When my nursing procedure had been completed satisfactorily, the usual questionnaire commenced: Cornelius Brendan Aloysius Brannigan, age 46 years, occupation — shepherd. The dulcet voice gave the answers to all the personal queries, until the one that proved embarrassing for him,

"Your religion, please, Con?"

Con fidgeted uneasily, blushed then spluttered some excuse about not being bothered with anything like that and that he had not done for many a year.

His wife, still treadling and stitching laughed mockingly and said, "Why can't you tell her the truth? Why can't you admit that you belong to that crowd who believe that nobody is going to heaven but themselves?"

I ventured to glance across at the faded ginger head bent low over her material and inquired rather timorously, "Which crowd is that, please, Mrs Brannigan?"

Mrs Brannigan, without raising her head replied, "Them there Catholics who can sin against God every day of their lives. Then they go to their confession and imagine that everything is straight with the Lord until they feel like doing the self-same thing, over and over again."

She followed this homily with an order to take the used water outside and dispose of it down the drain. I answered very quietly, "Yes, Mrs Brannigan." It was while obeying this command that I discovered the water supply to the cottage was obtained from a tap in the yard. Their only toilet was situated a few yards from the back door.

This rather spartan, hygienic system placed me in a very awkward position. Much as I wanted to escape from the house, without further involvement with Con's wife, I knew that some suggestions concerning toilet arrangements were essential. My offer to provide a urinal, commode and wheelchair was met with the now familiar, discourteous pose. Head bent over her sewing material, right foot moving forwards and backwards, she replied rudely, "Oh you can fetch what you like; he is all yours. As long as you know it is your job to empty the commode and lift him into the wheelchair and out of it."

Almost inaudibly I whispered, "Yes, Mrs Brannigan."

With the necessary equipment installed in 2 Hillfoot Cottages, one would quite naturally assume that life for every one concerned should have become, at least, a little easier. On the contrary, however, conditions became much more complicated. Each morning Con was washed, shaved, dressed and lifted from his uncomfortable bed into the invalid carriage. Each evening, either myself or one of my colleagues paid a return call, to undress him and transfer the paralyzed shepherd back to his camp bed. A nurse detailed for late evening duties also visited to ensure that the patient was made as comfortable as possible for the night. All this involvement of work and travel, despite the fact that there were two hefty young men at home in the evenings, resulted in a deep feeling of frustration. This frustration was shared with nursing staff and the patient.

Alan and Reuben Brannigan were both tall, broad shouldered and ginger haired like their mother. They were agricultural workers on a nearby farm. If they happened to be indoors during the nurse's evening visit, they always made a hasty exit through the back door. Thus they avoided all contact with the nursing staff and with their helpless father.

Soon it became evident that the mobile chair was nearly always pushed outside the front door, regardless of the inclement weather conditions prevailing at that time. Neighbours on either side of Number Two, who displayed a deal more sympathy for the pathetic little man than his own family, would take him indoors. They fed him and generally cared for him until the nurse's return visit.

A request to the local multiple sclerosis society for help with this difficult problem was answered sympathetically. A wonderful couple, June and Ted Picthall offered their support. June and Ted and their two teenage daughters devoted all their spare time to the welfare of multiple sclerosis sufferers.

Every Friday evening Ted drove from his terraced

house in Helmsvale to Hillfoot Cottages. He collected Con, all his nursing aids and paraphernalia and transported them to his home in the small market town, situated on the fringe of the Lake District. It was in the company of this very happy family that Con now spent his weekends.

Saturday afternoons soon became the most enjoyable part of his otherwise miserable existence. Due to the ingenuity of these two voluntary workers, he was manipulated into a sitting position in the rear of their station wagon. His posture was secured by their adept arrangement of several cushions and pillows with two strong leather straps.

He was then conveyed by either husband or wife, accompanied by one of their daughters, through the familiar lanes, moorlands and fells. Once he had been able to survey his well-known territory, they journeyed deeper into the heart of Lakeland, along the narrow, winding roads that eventually led to Torver and Coniston.

Their weekly drive usually took them through the picturesque village of Hawkshead, the world of the famous poet, William Wordsworth, passing through Far and Near Sawrey, the wonderland of Beatrix Potter. Already the Lakeland daffodils were in bloom creating a golden pattern on the carpets of grassland. By complete contrast, snow still capped the high hills. A secluded spot at the side of Esthwaite Water was their favourite stopping place.

Under the shadow of the hedgerows the trio would participate in a tasty picnic snack before returning home. When Ted was in charge of the pleasurable outing a quick stop at the Woodside Inn was included in the itinerary.

Television was an additional source of enjoyment

for Con. During the weekends that he spent in the Picthall's normal, comfortable home he developed quite an interest in the sporting events. June and Ted approached Mrs Brannigan regarding the installation of a television set in 2 Hillfoot Cottages. They offered to pay all expenses involved. Mrs Brannigan's outburst frightened them half to death.

Nevertheless, the extraordinary couple tried to persuade her and calm her wrath by suggesting that she would be able to keep in touch with the world outside, by watching and listening to the news bulletins. Mrs Brannigan pointed her stubby finger at the bulky Bible underneath the aspidistra plant and announced vehemently, "Owt I want to know about is contained in that book there. And if more of yous paid attention to what's written in them pages, there would be a lot less evil and suffering in yon big world of yours, outside. There would that."

Probably because of the apathy manifested towards him by his immediate family, Con refused to ask for his commode. Incontinence, therefore, became a major problem. His speech slurred to such an extent that it was almost impossible to understand what he was trying to say.

In spite of our combined efforts, six months following my initial visit and four months following confirmation of his diagnosis, Doctor Wardle, June, Ted and myself reluctantly admitted defeat. We realized that the only course left open to us was Con's early admission to Meadowlands Hospital, the local geriatric unit situated on the outskirts of Helmsvale. Doctor Wardle felt that the 46-year-old shepherd, who had spent the greatest part of his life in the fells and moorlands, would probably succumb to claustrophobia, if nothing more sophisticated claimed his life.

Con Brannigan's replacement was a big, beefy, florid faced man. As he herded his sheep through the lanes, with the aid of Ben and the other little collie, he tried to create the impression that the territory belonged solely to him and his Herdwick flocks. He seemed to go out of his way to delay motorists for as long as possible, by deliberately keeping the animals scattered over the narrow thoroughfare. Instead of the quiet greeting, "It's a mucky auld mornin'", I generally received a most ungracious order like, "Pull into the side, will you? If you happen to kill one of these with your motor you'll know about it. You will that."

I can honestly say that I really did miss Con a lot, although it was a great relief to be released from those increasingly frustrating calls to the Brannigan household. I visited the little Irish shepherd in the geriatric unit, perhaps two or three times. However, life goes on. New patients were admitted to my visiting register from time to time.

Many of them recovered. Others less fortunate were at least able to spend their last days in their own homes, tended affectionately by their caring families. There were other patients, due to circumstances beyond their control, like Con, who were admitted to hospital on a long-term basis to spend their remaining time on earth in the company of strangers on whom they were absolutely dependent.

After a few months of dealing with new situations and problems in my working sphere, Con Brannigan became one of many memories of those patients who came and went.

Chapter 3
Bernadette the shepherdess

Bernadette Soubirous was born on 7 January 1844 at the Boly Mill in Lourdes, a small town situated in the foothills of the Pyrenees. She was the eldest child of François and Louise Soubirous. Louise was unable to feed her baby daughter, because of a burning accident she had had earlier in her life. So Bernadette was sent to be wet nursed by a farmer's wife in Bartres, a village sited in a valley two miles north of Lourdes.

The young farmer and his wife had recently lost an infant son and the Soubirous child took the place of the deceased youngster. Madame Marie Lagues, the foster mother, promised to provide Bernadette with a mother's love that would never die. It was in the Lagues home, known as the Burg Maison, that the little girl spent the first two years of her life.

François Soubirous was the local miller. Unfortunately, his managerial ability left a lot to be desired. Both he and his wife were illiterate. They were also particularly fond of entertaining their customers to wine drinking sessions, instead of ensuring that their clientele paid their outstanding bills.

Due to this slipshod manner of conducting their business and the rather poor economic climate prevailing in their country at that time, by the summer of 1854, Monsieur and Madame Soubirous found themselves without a mill and without a home.

There were four surviving children of the marriage, two girls aged 13 and 10 years and two younger sons. The civil authorities housed the ill-fated family in a disused prison in the rue des Petits Fossés. This dilapidated building had been declared unfit to accommodate local convicted criminals. The cachot, or cell, allocated to François and Louise was situated at the end of a long flagged passage that opened into a yard. The yard contained a manure depot and the overflows from several lavatories in the vicinity.

It was a low, damp room four yards by five with a flagged stone floor and an open fireplace along the wall. The small, barred windows looked out on to the manure depot. A crude wooden table, a few stools, three beds and a trunk containing some clothing, were the family's worldly possessions. Living under these circumstances must have been soul-destroying. It was not uncommon for the two young Soubirous boys, Jean-Marie and Justin to eat candle wax from the parish church floor. François earned a meagre wage as a casual labourer while Louise went out cleaning and engaged herself in seasonal work in the fields.

During the summer of 1855, an epidemic of cholera swept through Lourdes. Bernadette was stricken with the disease. She was given the only treatment known at that time — rubbing the back of the sufferer with straw, until the skin peeled. However drastic the therapy may have been, at least the 11-year-old girl recovered, if only partially. From then onwards, Bernadette was subject to asthmatic attacks. Often as she laid in bed in the damp and offensive cachot, her severely laboured breathing depriving her of sleep, she wept bitterly about the dreadful poverty that her family were forced to endure.

Due to the wretched conditions that existed in the Soubirous household, Bernadette, at the age of 13, returned to her foster mother at Bartrès. It was there that she worked very hard as a shepherdess in the sheepfolds surrounding the village. With the help of Marie Lagues, she tried to learn sufficient catechism to enable her to take her first holy communion. After six months, she requested to return home. Bernadette was 14 years old when she returned to the appalling cachot overrun with vermin and stench. She was practically illiterate and as far as prayers were concerned could recite only the Pater Noster, Ave Maria and the Creed. It could not be claimed, therefore, that she was a particularly pious girl.

The apparitions

On 11 February 1858, Bernadette Soubirous pleaded with her mother to be allowed to go wood gathering with her sister Toinette and a school friend named Baloume Abadie. Louise, concerned for her elder daughter's health, at first refused. However, when Bernadette donned her capulet and promised faithfully not to remove her sabots and stockings, Louise relented. The three girls set off at a running pace on that very cold, foggy morning.

They ran along the woodland path by the side of the Savy mill stream towards the bank of the River Gave. Bernadette asked Toinette and Baloume if they would like to see where the water from the millstream joined the Gave. When they said they would, the happy trio followed the canal and found themselves in a rather bleak spot directly in front of the grotto Massabielle (which means 'old hump'). It was an unofficial rubbish dump.

Toinette and Baloume removed their sabots and stockings, threw them to the opposite side of the grotto, then waded across. Bernadette leaned against a rock at the side. It was 12 noon and the Angelus bells were ringing when she heard a noise like a strong breeze blowing. She felt afraid and decided to break her earlier promise to her mother. She had already removed one sabot when a similar sound occurred. Bernadette turned towards the meadow and was quite surprised to find the trees were not moving. The bushes and small shrubs at the side of the grotto, however, were swaying to and fro.

When the sound returned for a third time, she looked towards the grotto. Underneath the highest opening, the brambles were tossing furiously. Everything else remained perfectly still. Behind the brambles stood a lady. She was wearing a white dress with a blue sash. The lady held a yellow rosary and on each of her feet was a rose of the same colour.

Bernadette rubbed her eyes, looked again at the lady who appeared to be smiling. Although conscious of some slight degree of fear at this extraordinary manifestation, the little girl had no desire to run away. She removed her rosary from her pocket, but when she tried to cross herself, her head fell backwards. The lady made the sign of the cross then commenced to pass the large beads through her fingers. She did not, however, move her lips. With all traces of fright vanished, Bernadette crossed herself and recited the rosary. When the five Pater Nosters and 50 Aves were completed, the lady retired into the niche in the rock and disappeared.

Toinette and Baloume, each carrying a bundle of wood on her back, were astonished on their return to find the ailing 14-year-old kneeling in the water and gazing at the niche high in the rock. Their calling and throwing pebbles at the inert figure were completely ineffective. Toinette cried out thinking that her elder sister was dead, but Baloume calmed her friend by stating that dead people were always found lying down.

When Bernadette recovered from the ecstatic state, the girls divided the wood into three equal parts and set off for home, each carrying a bundle. They took the path over the hill of Espeluges which was extremely steep; yet Bernadette hurried upwards with no apparent sign of breathlessness. This surprised her two companions.

On questioning her why she had knelt in the water and stared fixedly at the grotto, Bernadette eventually confided in her sister regarding the apparition. She made Toinette promise solemnly that there would be no mention of the incident to their parents. Toinette did not, however, keep her promise. The result was a severe thrashing administered to both girls by their mother who instructed them, in no uncertain manner, never to go to the grotto Massabielle again.

On the following Sunday, 14 February, an overwhelming impulse to return to the grotto engulfed Bernadette, but the memory of the recent beating remained very vivid, both mentally and physically. Toinette and Baloume came to her rescue and pleaded with Madame Soubirous to permit them to visit the grotto. They promised most sincerely to take care of the elder girl and to ensure that she did not go into the water.

Once again, Louise relented and the trio accompanied by several other young girls, hurried down the zigzag path towards the bleak spot where the Savy millstream joined the River Gave. Bernadette had with her a bottle containing holy water to sprinkle over the vision should it appear.

On reaching the Massabielle rock, each girl knelt down and began to recite the rosary. As soon as Bernadette had completed the first 10 Aves, she noticed the lady wearing the white dress and blue sash and carrying a yellow rosary. The young shepherdess threw the holy water at the vision. She invited the strange lady to stay if she came from God and if she did not, please would she go away.

When the entire bottle of holy water had been sprinkled wildly, the vision remained and appeared to bow and smile. Only Bernadette, none of the others present, nor any person at any time has been recorded as having seen or heard anything unusual at the grotto Massabielle. When Bernadette completed her rosary, the lady again retired into the niche and vanished.

All the girls assembled were greatly distressed about the Soubirous girl's condition. Her white face, her eyes fixed on the grotto and her motionless body, was a phenomenon that none of these young ladies had ever experienced. They shouted loudly at her; they shook her frail body forcefully, to no avail. Some members of the group ran to the nearby Savy mill to get help. Toinette and a few others remained with the impassive figure.

Baloume went at break-neck speed to the cachot to alert Madame Soubirous. First to arrive on the scene were the Savy miller's wife, Madame Nicolau and her son, Antoine. Both these individuals witnessed the 14-year-old girl kneeling on the cold, wet floor. Her eyes were wide open and fixed on the niche in the rock, her face was ashen. Tears streamed down the pallid cheeks, yet she was smiling.

Considerable effort on the part of the good lady and her son were required, to remove the unconscious girl and carry her to their home. It was almost an hour later that consciousness was regained and the colour restored to the ashen face.

Louise Soubirous escorted her daughter from the Savy mill to the cachot, rebuking her about her unusual behaviour. Louise was more than a little concerned regarding the small crowd of people who had gathered to look at the young girl whose strange experiences were already being publicized throughout the community. Louise vowed that there would be no further excursions to the grotto.

Madame Milhet, a wealthy lady of some social standing in Lourdes, however, called at the wretched cachot on the following Wednesday evening. She suggested that she should accompany young Bernadette to the grotto Massabielle the next morning, Thursday 18 February. Following a deal of coercion, Louise and François Soubirous eventually consented to the proposal.

Madame Milhet carried a blessed candle. Her friend Madame Peyret carried pen, writing paper and ink. On arrival at the bleak grotto, the two adults and the child began the recitation of the rosary. Almost immediately, the little girl announced that the lady had appeared. Madame Milhet urged her to ask the lady what it was she wanted. On that occasion, the young shepherdess did not go into ecstasy. She took the pen and paper, proceeded towards the niche in the rock, then stopped. She claimed that the lady had gestured to her not to go any further.

Bernadette then requested the name of the mysterious lady, who she referred to as 'Aquero', a word meaning 'that' in the patois dialect. Aquero did not reveal her identity on that occasion, although it was the first time that there is any record of her having spoken. Aquero invited Bernadette to go to the grotto each day for the following two weeks. The little girl replied that she would, provided her parents would grant their permission.

Her Aquero also requested that she go tell the priests to have a chapel built on the rock. She is also recorded as having informed Bernadette that she could not promise her happiness in this world but in the next. The apparition's disappearance was different on that Thursday morning. She rose upwards and vanished into the roof of the niche.

Madame Milhet emerges as a person endowed with outstanding persuasive powers. She insisted that Louise should escort her daughter to the grotto Massabielle. Quite early, on the morning of Friday 19 February, Bernadette, her mother, her godmother, Madame Barnarde and some other family friends wended their way along the zigzag slope.

On arrival at the rock, each person kneeled down and the rosary was commenced. Bernadette went into ecstasy almost immediately and again there was panic because of the deathly appearance of the little girl. It is written that Louise actually screamed out a prayer to God, beseeching him not to take her beloved child from her. At the end of half an hour, however, Bernadette had recovered her normal appearance. She stated that the lovely lady had merely smiled at her in silence.

Next morning which was extremely cold and frosty, quite a number of local people knelt and witnessed the 14-year-old girl in an ecstatic state hold a lighted candle in her left hand and a rosary in her right. Among the silent and solemn assembly was a rather sceptical doctor who suspected an attack of hysteria. He approached the motionless figure and checked her pulse and respiration, which he later registered as being within normal limits.

Varying accounts of these extraordinary events in the small town had begun to gain momentum. People from surrounding areas, in order to satisfy their curiosity, were making their way to Lourdes. One small section of the community profoundly worried about the current local events was the police constabulary.

Following her visit to her familiar grotto on Sunday 21 February, Bernadette Soubirous attended Mass in the parish church. As she left the austere building, she was startled when the hood of her capulet was tugged and she found herself being led away. The police official conducted her to the house of the chief constable Monsieur Dominique Jacomet. Monsieur Jacomet made notes as she talked. When the statement was read back, Bernadette listened carefully and corrected the gentleman several times saying, "I did not say that." At the end of 45 minutes, some local people gathered outside. The door was kicked and there were threats of breaking it down if the little girl was not released. Monsieur Jacomet extracted a pledge from François Soubirous that he would prohibit his daughter from returning to the grotto.

The following morning Bernadette went back to school where she was already suffering great indignities. These included being spat upon and slapped across her face, not only by her school colleagues but also by their parents. She had not attended Mass that morning neither had she been to the grotto.

During her frugal lunch, she begged her parent's permission to visit her favourite spot. This time they refused to succumb to her pleas. To ensure that she went directly back to school, her mother escorted her as far as the gate. Bernadette waited until her mother was out of sight, then the overwhelming sensation came again. She ran all the way down to the Massabielle rock but her Aquero did not appear.

François and Louise discussed at great length the mysterious behaviour of their eldest child. Had their daughter been chosen by God or was she indeed insane? At the end of much deliberation, they concluded that they would not dissuade Bernadette from going to the grotto.

It was, therefore, with her parents blessing that she set out before dawn on Tuesday 23 February. The very early hour did not deter the local people from accompanying her. In the presence of approximately 100 people, she went into ecstasy with all the familiar signs. She claimed that the lady taught her a prayer that she was to recite every day for the rest of her life.

On Wednesday 24 February, the number of witnesses had doubled. Spellbound they observed the young girl's every movement. She knelt for a few moments before the trance overwhelmed her. Something different happened. Bernadette's eyes filled with tears. Still in a kneeling position, she made her way into the hollow of the grotto, conversing with her strange lady all the while. Backwards and forwards from the interior to the exterior several times she went. At intervals she would lower her frail body to kiss the ground. Later Bernadette stated that Aquero had instructed her, in her native patois to pray for the conversion of sinners and kiss the ground in penitence for sinners.

Thursday 25 February found the customary gathering at the grotto Massabielle. They watched the young girl moving on her knees and kissing the ground. Those kneeling nearest to her could hear her whispering, "Penitence" over and over again. The scene changed as Bernadette scratched the ground at various points. Between these rather peculiar actions, the pallid face would raise and the large, open eyes would stare at the niche in the rock, before resuming the process.

After many attempts of clawing at the earth, finally the little girl was seen to scoop some water in her hands, drink it, then splash some of the water over her face. Explanations later revealed that her Aquero had instructed her to drink from the fountain. As there was no fountain visible, "I kept asking Aquero to direct me and eventually her instructions led me to the spring."

Bernadette's clawing at the soil, her shuffling around on her hands and knees and her murmurings led the majority of the bystanders to believe that she was quite mad. As soon as her ecstasy ended, Bernadette walked quietly away. Rumours concerning the happenings at the grotto Massabielle were rife. In a great many instances, they were grossly exaggerated.

Chief Constable Jacomet decided to seek help with what he considered to be a daily nuisance. He approached the Imperial Prosecutor of Lourdes, Monsieur Dutour, who summoned François and

Bernadette Soubirous to his office. However, François did not attend, so Louise chaperoned her daughter on the fearful occasion.

The meeting proved to be a repetition of the previous Sunday. Bernadette's statement was read back to her by the Imperial Prosecutor; she again replied, "I did not say that, Sir."

In a most irate manner, the gentleman threatened the two females with instant imprisonment. Louise wept bitterly and trembled with fright. A number of local men rescued the unfortunate pair by declaring loudly their intention of breaking down the door. Monsieur Dutour decided to postpone the affair until the next day.

Shortly after the first apparition, Bernadette had in the confessionals informed one of the priests in Lourdes of her experience. At his request, she had given her consent that he should mention the incident to his superior, Abbé Peyramale. The clergy, however, ignored the whole business. On the morning of Friday 26 February, the young girl knelt at the grotto, prayed and performed her acts of penitence. There was no ecstasy and no lady appeared.

However when Bernadette returned to the grotto that weekend, her lady did appear. Her trance-like state no longer frightened people, as more and more came to see her in her ecstasy. Despite torrential rain, 2,000 people assembled on the Sunday morning. Among the large gathering was a local policeman, sent there by his superiors to keep order. As the young girl kissed the ground, he was overcome and commanded that all present should follow her example.

Bernadette Soubirous decided to call on the parish priest of Lourdes after the tenth apparition, which had occurred on that Saturday morning. Abbé Peyramale, renowned for his detestation of heresy, visions and the like, was not impressed. He frowned as he listened to the 14-year-old peasant girl talking about a beautiful lady, dressed in white, standing in a niche in the rock.

When she told him that the mysterious lady had instructed her to tell the clergy to build a chapel on the rock, he scowled and inquired who this strange lady was and what was her name. Bernadette answered that she did not know the lady's name. Abbé Peyramale told the girl that he considered it very peculiar that she had not asked the lady to reveal her identity. Bernadette replied that she had asked her Aquero for her name but she had smiled instead of answering the question.

At the end of the discourse, the Abbé made no attempt to conceal his wrath. He shouted at the young girl, "Find out who she is and if she thinks she has the right to order clergy to build chapels. If she has this right tell her to prove it by making the rose bush at the grotto flower immediately."

During the Sunday morning apparition, when a vast number of inhabitants of the area kissed the ground on the orders of the emotional policeman, Bernadette kept her promise to the stern Abbé Peyramale. She asked the lady her name and to prove her presence by making the rose bush flower. However, she returned to the angry man's house to inform him once more that Aquero had merely smiled at the request.

As she left the parish church after hearing Mass, Bernadette was arrested again and taken to the house of the local magistrate where she was interrogated yet again. She was once more threatened with imprisonment if she ventured near the grotto Massabielle ever again. Following the intimidation, she was permitted to go home.

However, despite this ordeal, the following morning which was the first day of March, in the presence of approximately 2,000 people, Bernadette, kneeling in front of the rock, went into ecstasy and prayed in her customary manner.

The early morning of Tuesday 2 March brought an even greater number of people to the grotto. When Bernadette regained consciousness on that occasion, she seemed very troubled. She told her parents that Aquero had given her a further message for the clergy. She was to inform them that Aquero desired people to go there in procession. And once again she requested that a chapel be erected on the rock.

Standing between her Aunt Bernarde and her Aunt Basile in the ascetic reception room in the presbytery, her legs shook with fear of Abbé Peyramale. He stood in the middle of the floor scowling at the three females before him. Bernadette delivered the message concerning the procession. The priest's anger knew no bounds. He called the girl a liar, a cheat and a downright trouble maker. Still shouting at the top of his voice, he asked her if she had discovered the odd lady's name. When the terrified youngster answered that she had not, he yelled, "Well, you must ask her." He opened the door, ushered the three frightened people through it, then banged it loudly shut.

The Abbé was deeply concerned. The police were already exerting pressure on him to use his influence in an attempt to halt the ever increasing numbers of people attending the grotto. They indicated to the Abbé the hazards posed by enormous gatherings in such inappropriate surroundings.

Cautions from the local magistrate and the furious parish priest had obviously been completely ignored by the Soubirous girl, for on Wednesday 3 March, she visited the grotto Massabielle as usual. Her vision, however, did not appear. A crowd of a few thousand shared her disappointment. She went to school in tears.

At lunchtime, however, she sensed Aquero tugging at her heart strings, a sensation that she now knew so well. Accompanied by an aunt and cousin and taking a completely different route, she went back to her favourite spot. Aquero was already there. Bernadette prayed and yet again asked the lady her name. As always a sweet smile was the only response.

Thursday 4 March was to be the last day of the fortnight. It was market day in Lourdes. From daybreak, thousands of people, of all age groups were thronging into the small town. They trudged along the woodland paths and across the meadow towards the grotto Massabielle. Not only were police reinforcements employed, but the army was alerted as an extra precaution. The great mass of humanity confined itself to the area surrounding the Massabielle rock, leaving the town empty and ghost-like. Bernadette, because of a bereavement of one of her cousins, had not arrived by seven o'clock which was quite unusual.

Monsieur Jacomet, instead of his hitherto thwarting her visits, called at the cachot to escort her to her haunt. She arrived and commenced her rosary recitation. Her ecstatic state took over shortly afterwards. It lasted for one hour, during which time, Monsieur Jacomet observed closely, her every smile, her changes of countenance and, indeed, each movement she made.

When questioned why she had been so clumsy in making the sign of the cross at the end of her rosary recital and only achieved it at the third attempt, she explained that she was only able to cross herself when Aquero did.

After that particular apparition, which was the fifteenth, there was a perpetual stream of people wending their way to the cachot in the rue des Petits Fossés. Their requests for her to bless pious objects were firmly refused. The little girl informed the well-meaning people that she would pray for their intentions.

A determined Bernadette, paid yet another call to the equally obstinate Abbé Peyramale. She informed him that although she was still unaware of the mysterious lady's identity and the rose bush at the side of the rock had not yet flowered, she still wanted the chapel built on the rock. His curt reply was not dissimilar to his former one, "Tell her to produce the money, then."

From that day until 25 March, young Bernadette Soubirous left the grotto alone. Not only did she cease to go there, she never mentioned the place. She had claimed the attention of a great number of people for a rather brief period. To all intents and purposes she had retired into the obscurity from which she had emerged. There were, however, a few people who continued to pray and light candles at the grotto Massabielle.

Gossip concerning previous incidents at the grotto was widespread. There were those who claimed inexplicable cures at the rock. A court case in which the Soubirous family was accused of accepting money had been dismissed. Abbé Peyramale felt a sense of triumph as he read these various accounts in the local newspaper. He decided that the unfortunate affair had, at last, reached its conclusion. At least, he very much hoped so.

Three weeks elapsed before the young shepherdess sensed the pulling at her heart strings. Aquero was calling her back to the spot where it had all began. It was five o'clock in the morning of March 25. She rose and informed her parents that she was going down to the grotto.

When she arrived there, she found the bleak spot ablaze with light. Her lovely lady stood in the niche where she had originally appeared. Later, Bernadette stated that Aquero was so close, on that occasion, that it would have been almost possible to stretch out a hand and touch her. Ecstasy began during the recital of the first few Aves. On completion of her rosary, Bernadette, for the very first time since the commencement of the apparitions, stood while in ecstasy and moved towards the hollow in the rock. She remained standing and whispering as if conversing with the vision.

She repeated her request to the lady to reveal her identity. Three times she reiterated her question but her vision continued to respond with the usual, sweet smile. Bernadette ventured to ask the lady, yet again, who she really was. At the end of her fourth entreaty, her Aquero raised her eyes upwards, parted her clasped hands, letting her arms drop, then rejoined her hands and in patois dialect announced, "Que soy era 'Immaculada Councepciou'" ("I am the Immaculate Conception"). The strange sounding term meant nothing to the semi-illiterate, peasant girl. She kept repeating the two peculiar words over and over again as she made her way quickly to the presbytery.

Abbé Peyramale was not pleased to find the Soubirous girl back on his doorstep. In her utter naiveté, she looked into the stern face of the man, who normally treated her so harshly. She informed him that her Aquero had, at last, revealed her identity and her name was 'Immaculate Conception'. The priest was astonished and dumbfounded. His perplexity was due to the fact that the doctrine concerning the Immaculate Conception had not been proclaimed by Pope Pius IX until four years previously. It was highly improbable that the peasant youngster standing before him had ever heard those two words spoken by anyone, except the vision that she claimed to converse with at the grotto Massabielle. Abbé Peyramale wasted no time in contacting his superior, Bishop Laurance, at Tarbes. He waited impatiently for the venerable gentleman's reply. Until this reply arrived, he decided to make no mention to anyone about the peasant girl's disclosure.

Easter Sunday and Monday of the following week produced a few thousand strong crowd at the grotto. Bernadette did not go to her favourite haunt, however, until Wednesday 7 April. On that occasion, a most outstanding incident occurred.

The sceptical and irreligious Doctor Dozous was among the 1,200 people present. He noticed that the lighted candle which Bernadette held as she prayed, had slipped down, and its flame was licking the inside of her wrist and hand. As voices shouted in horror that she was in danger of being burned, Doctor Dozous ordered them to be quiet. Fifteen minutes elapsed, yet Bernadette remained motionless and oblivious to the fact that the flame was engulfing her hand.

When her trance-like state ended and the candle dropped to the ground, only then did the doctor approach her. He examined her hand and wrist, then announced loudly that there was no trace of burn marks. He had the candle relit, touched her lightly with its flame and she screamed out with pain, pulling her hand away as she said, "You are burning me." Doctor Dozous became not only one of the most zealous believers in the Lourdes apparitions, but also a mighty defender of Bernadette Soubirous.

Bernadette visited the grotto only once after that extraordinary event. Her absence at the Massabielle rock may have been partly due to the pressure imposed upon herself and her family by the civil authorities. She had been confined to bed for one week because of an asthmatic attack. When she recovered sufficiently, she spent two weeks away from Lourdes, in Cauterets, where she had relatives. She received her first holy communion on 3 June, the feast of Corpus Christi.

Her absence from the grotto did nothing to alleviate the ever increasing throngs of people milling around it. Reports of happenings at the Massabielle rock were numerous and, naturally, very variable. Exhibitionists, tricksters and the like moved on to the scene with resulting chaos.

On her return from Cauterets, Bernadette Soubirous was again subject to lengthy and gruelling interrogations by the police officials. Once again, they threatened her with imprisonment. They continued to accuse her of accepting money for services as a faith healer – an accusation that she forcefully denied. Finally, they decided that the most appropriate method of disposal of this source of

43

tumult in their midst was her committal to a mental institution.

There is little doubt that their plan would have succeeded but for the intervention of Abbé Peyramale. He informed the officials that the youngster was not the cause of the confusion existing in their midst. He instructed them that they would have to tread over his dead body, if any of them dared to touch as much as a hair on her head.

In order to make the grotto inaccessible, fences had been erected but these were pulled down and dismantled with amazing alacrity. Finally, the entire area of the Massabielle rock was declared forbidden ground. Trespassers would be prosecuted as would any one discovered taking water from the spring. A stout barrier encircling a wide area bore notices to the effect that it was an illegal place of worship.

After 17 apparitions, it was three months before Bernadette felt the familiar sensation again. The time was eight o'clock in the morning of 16 July. She walked towards her heaven on earth, escorted by her Aunt Lucille. Because of the high barricade, they were unable to see the actual rock as they knelt on the grass in the meadow, situated on the opposite side of the river. Bernadette removed her rosary from her pocket and commenced her recital. When she had completed a few Aves she smiled and said, "She is here, smiling at us, over the fence." Her ecstasy lasted 20 minutes, then her Aquero vanished forever.

Bernadette never felt the desire to visit the grotto Massabielle again. She is quoted as having said, "I felt as though I was actually at the grotto. I did not see the River or the fence that separated us. Aquero never looked more beautiful."

On 5 October that year, Napoleon the third emperor of France issued a command which allowed free access to the famous grotto Massabielle.

Meanwhile Monsignor Laurance, Bishop of Tarbes, had elected a committee of some highly scholastic gentlemen, consisting mainly of members of the medical profession and some eminent clergymen. A large number of witnesses were requested to give testimony regarding reports of inexplicable cures.

Bernadette was subjected to intensive physical and mental examinations. There was a thorough analysis of her environmental background, undertaken by distinguished members of the fact-finding assembly. On 7 December, Monsignor Laurance summoned Bernadette Soubirous once more before the commission of inquiry, presided over by himself. When the young girl repeated the vision of 25 March and imitated the gestures and attitude of the lady, who had declared that she was the Immaculate Conception, he was so moved with emotion that tears spilled down his face.

It was not until January 1862 that the judgement was proclaimed. A famous document, Mandement de Monsignor Laurance, detailed the experiences of Bernadette Soubirous as related personally and supported by reliable witnesses and concluded that accounts reported were genuine. It was proposed that a copy of the document be submitted to the Sovereign Pontiff, Pope Pius IX.

Publicity overwhelmed the Soubirous family. Abbé Peyramale, in an attempt to save them further embarrassment, was influential in having them removed from the dreadful cachot. They were rehoused in the old Gras mill sited at a point where the Lapaca meets the Gave. In the year 1863, François and Louise Soubirous rented the Lacade mill.

Bernadette lived there for a very short time, as Abbé Peyramale had already persuaded the Sisters of Christian Instruction and Charity to accept her as a boarder in their local hospice. She was not received graciously by the nuns who were aware of her inferior educational standards and the public attention that surrounded her.

On 7 July 1866, Bernadette entered the order of Sisters of Christian Instruction and Charity at their mother house in Nevers. Before leaving Lourdes, she paid her farewell visit to the Massabielle rock and wept as she gazed at the plaster image of her Aquero in the niche in the rock. As she wiped the tears from her eyes, she kissed the piece of rock underneath the rose bush, then walked away quickly without a backward glance.

Bernadette Soubirous was an extremely unhealthy 21-year-old, when she entered the novitiate at Nevers. She underwent considerable difficulty in trying to come to terms with the demands imposed upon her by the religious life. Mother Marie Therese Vauzou, who was mistress of novices at that time, may well have been responsible for some of the hardship the young novice was forced to endure. The older nun, from time to time, displayed outward signs of jealousy towards her new charge from Lourdes. On the other hand, however, she may well have found Bernadette exasperating. In addition to her ill health and severe lack of talents, she was a most stubborn and touchy individual. She did not conform easily to the devotional regime prescribed by the order. She liked to conduct her prayers in her own unconventional manner.

Therefore, Bernadette's life inside the convent was probably as difficult to bear as her previous impecunious existence had been. Despite the frustrations and humiliation associated with her religious life, Bernadette spent the remaining 13 years of her life at Nevers. As Sister Marie Bernarde (her name in religion), at the age of 35, she died on 16 April 1879. Her human remains have been preserved and can be viewed at Saint Bernadette's shrine in the convent of Saint Gildard at Nevers.

The basilica of the Immaculate Conception, an architectural masterpiece in thirteenth century Gothic style, was designed by Hippolyte Durand. Its construction involved nine years of hard labour which included the hewing away of tons of rock from the precipitous Espeluges.

On the feast of the Assumption, 15 August 1871, this splendid house of worship was officially opened and blessed. It was not consecrated until the second of July 1876. It would have been impossible for Bernadette Soubirous to envisage the magnificent chapel on the rock when she was campaigning for it so zealously. She visited Lourdes in May 1866 and attended the first mass to be celebrated in the crypt underneath the grand basilica. Monsignor Laurance officiated at the ceremony. Before leaving the hospice for her return to Nevers, she prayed at the grotto Massabielle for the very last time. The experience proved extremely traumatic for the 23-year-old nun, as she wept uncontrollably and unashamedly.

After a period of 54 years and eight months from her death, the little shepherdess was exalted to the saintly ranks, when Pope Pius XI conducted her canonization ceremony on 8 December 1933.

Chapter 4
An invitation

Lourdes had been the subject of a great many sermons and personal testimonies, which I had listened to attentively in the past. Some individuals became quite emotional, and in some cases I felt moved dangerously close to ecstasy as they related and obviously relived their visits to various venues of worship in Lourdes. Yet, my imagination was often completely captured by illustrious reports of the grotto, the basilicas, the baths and the extraordinary sensations of spiritual elation experienced by people who had recently returned from the famous spot.

Moreover, on three different occasions, I queued for lengthy periods outside a downtown cinema in Belfast, for the privilege of obtaining a seat and crying my way through 'The Song of Bernadette'. This emotive film has been based on the book of the same title by Franz Werfel. The latter was a German Jewish gentleman who sought refuge in Lourdes during the Second World War.

On reflection, the Lourdes affair had been arousing my curiosity for a great many years prior to my initial visit to the strange town in the foothills of the Pyrenees. The opportunity to tend the travelling sick did not present itself until a few months prior to the departure of the Lancaster Diocesan annual pilgrimage in 1962.

Ironically, Con Brannigan and Father Alfred

Brocklebank, the priest in charge of our local church, were two of the most unlikely characters to be slightly interested in Lourdes, yet they were entirely responsible for my involvement in the care of sick pilgrims. Reverend Alfred Brocklebank, parish priest of Saint Mary's Catholic Church in Helmsvale, was of average height, slender build and slightly stooped. His stoop and thick, snow white hair gave him the appearance of being older than his 54 years.

He was completely different in character from the priests I remembered in Ireland. These gentlemen seemed to consider it essential to keep their parishioners constantly aware of the flames of hell. Father Brocklebank, by contrast, appeared to be more interested in the effects of the prevailing weather conditions on growing crops and the current price of farm produce, than he was in the salvation of souls. He was a local man from farming stock and immensely popular with all members of the community, regardless of denomination. Because of his keen interest in agricultural activities, I often considered the traditional, black suit and dog collar totally unsuitable garb for him. I felt that he would have been more at ease in baggy tweeds, battered trilby and gum boots.

Occasionally, he visited my home on his way back from chaplain duties in Meadowlands Hospital which housed a few hundred Cumbrian geriatric patients. It was during the course of one of these casual visits that I realized how very inaccurate my assessment of his character had been. I discovered underneath the rustic mien, a man of outstanding acumen, a paragon of virtue and a most dedicated priest who worked assiduously for the benefit of humanity without a trace of sanctimoniousness.

He had just swallowed a mouthful of lemon meringue pie, his favourite delicacy, and with his cup of tea half way to his mouth, he said quite suddenly, "I was wondering if you would like to do a spot of nursing in the Lourdes pilgrimage."

Father Brocklebank seemed to have an unwritten rule that prevented him from asking outright for help with church or charity work of any kind. He always 'wondered' if the person concerned 'would like to do a spot of' this or that or whatever.

His wondering met with excellent results. All his church functions were financially successful. The interior of Saint Mary's was polished until it sparkled; the colourful shrubs and flowers surrounding the church and presbytery were arranged from season to season, so that there were always blooms to admire. These achievements were all due to the voluntary efforts of the men and women, young and not so young, within his parish.

Although my feelings regarding the proposed deal were somewhat confused, I agreed to join the pilgrimage work force. The priest-cum-farmer gave me his familiar answer to a favourable acquiescence, "Good lass, I knew I could rely on you."

Without allowing any time for questioning, he explained his reason for the unusual request. During his chaplain duties in Meadowlands Hospital, he had discovered among the crippled bodies and minds, a youngish man named Con Brannigan, who was completely paralyzed. Con occupied a corner bed and, to quote Father Brocklebank, "stares at the same piece of wall, all day every day; a witness to his own physical and mental decay".

At that point, I interrupted and indicated that I was fairly well-acquainted with Con and knew him to be a completely godless person. As the sick people who travelled half way across Europe in search of a miraculous cure for their ailments must be endowed with strong spiritual convictions, surely to transport such a man would be a futile task.

The priest informed me that faith is a priceless gift. Individuals who are bereft of faith are blameless. They should be helped in every way possible and life is much too short to adopt attitudes. As for a miraculous cure, the thought had not entered his mind. For some time past, he had been concerning himself about the possibility of relieving the overwhelming boredom that surrounded Con. The Lourdes trip seemed to be the only solution, providing he could find a nurse to accompany the sorely afflicted man.

In other words, Father Brocklebank, after giving the matter a great deal of thought, had begun the process of arranging the only type of holiday possible for Con Brannigan. The short and unexpected homily made me realize that my explanation of the little shepherd's admission to hospital should be expressed with the utmost discretion.

Father Brocklebank puffed contentedly at his pipe as he listened to my abridged account of Mrs Brannigan's insensibility and hypocrisy. The puckered brow, slight frown and occasional twitch of face indicated my lack of diplomacy, in spite of great effort to disguise my personal opinion of the strange woman. A few moments later, probably quite unintentionally, Father Brocklebank made me feel very conscious of my dearth of Christian charity.

He commenced his softly spoken narration by stating that as a mere mortal, encumbered by all the shortcomings and failings of such creatures, he did not feel he was in a position to moralize about his fellow human beings. He remembered Mrs Brannigan from their primary school days and later as the vivacious redhead who had been the life and soul of the village where they lived. She belonged to a dairy farming family. Her parents used every threat within reason to oppose her marriage to Con, because of his habitual drinking. When she ultimately defied them and became the wife of the Irish shepherd, she had been cut off from her family without even the proverbial shilling.

Father Brocklebank relit his pipe, exhaled a cloud of smoke and continued, "Hetty's married life has been one of great sacrifice. Were it not for the fact that she is so clever with the needle, I shudder to think what might have happened to her and the children. Sharing her life with a husband whose earnings passed over the counter in the Woodside Inn week after week and the added fear that her two sons might follow their father's example, must have caused her great hardship and heartache. I understand that during the early days of their marriage, Con did try really hard to curb his drinking without success. He was always a lonely little soul. Nobody begrudged him a drink or two when he came down from the fells, if only he had been able to leave it at that. However, there but for the grace of God, go an awful lot of us. I have not seen Hetty for a great many years. I feel so sorry for her and Con and only wish that there was something more I could do to help them."

My new-found philanthropist informed me that all expenses involved in this strange, continental trip would be met by him and the parochial Lourdes sick fund. He supplied me with the name and address of the matron to the travelling sick. He also advised me to contact her as soon as possible. He further requested me to inform Con that he had been chosen as a sick pilgrim and find out if he wished to take advantage of the generous offer. If Con agreed to the proposal, then Father Brocklebank 'wondered' if I would like to pop out to Hillfoot Cottages and put Hetty in the picture.

While I was most decidedly disliking the idea of meeting Mrs Brannigan again, a different image of the unusual lady was beginning to emerge. Her almost incessant treadling and stitching, the scrubbed, flagged floor with the expertly woven peg rugs, the shining window panes, the thoroughly black leaded range and its mirror-like brass rail were all indications of the drudgery that Mrs Brannigan had been forced to endure, in order to maintain her independence.

I had visited her humble home at least twice daily for a period of six months and had failed to acknowledge the proud woman's pitiable existence. As soon as the priest departed, the sharp jolt that my conscience had just received, impelled me to proceed immediately towards that bed in one of the corners of the grey, austere building, Meadowlands Hospital.

Chapter 5
The reunion

The ward was painted a pretty pastel shade of blue. The beds were covered in matching blue counterpanes and the windows looked out on beautifully landscaped gardens. Certainly the hospital authorities had done their utmost to make the place as comfortable as possible; yet all around there was an emanation of human decay.

Men screamed and swore obscenely at no-one in particular. Some cried while others sang tunelessly. Those who were not mentally incapacitated read the local evening paper or books with the aid of magnifying glasses, while others listened to the radio with the aid of headphones.

Nurses of both sexes and all grades dashed from bed to bed endlessly. I did not envy them their chosen branch of our profession but admired their courage tremendously; an admiration which I still cherish for all nurses who opt to work in the geriatric departments. Surely it is in these wards that dedication to duty shines brightest. Rarely do these gallant bands of men and women enjoy the satisfaction of seeing their patients recover. Nevertheless, they continue to provide tender, loving care to the aged and chronically sick people who are often quite young, enabling them to live their last few years, months or weeks with dignity.

Con was strapped loosely in a wheelchair by his

bed in the corner. When the young male nurse escorted me towards him and offered me a seat, he eased the embarrassment considerably by saying,

"Oh, aye, Con, lad, you never said nowt about this, did you? I allus said you were a bit of a dark horse." He ruffled the dark wiry hair and left.

The little shepherd did not recognize me out of uniform and, in different circumstances, I would not have recognized him. The once, weather-beaten face was chalk white and the big, brown eyes were dull and lifeless. He squinted at the ceiling, then at the floor and finally at me. His multiple sclerosis had progressed considerably. Both arms lay clumsily across the special arm rests attached to his invalid chair.

I lifted a useless hand and held it while I told him who I was, then delivered my message without involving Father Brocklebank. Con made several attempts to answer but the severity of his speech impairment prevented him from doing so for quite some time.

After some minutes and much difficulty the slurred words tumbled out, "Och sure Nurse, I'd like to go right enough but I've got no money at all, at all."

When he had been reassured that he could safely forget about the financial side of the venture, his chalky white face seemed to brighten a little. He looked almost like the shepherd whose face brightened in the Woodside Inn, a few years previously, as he joined in the singing of 'It's a long way to Tipperary'.

In spite of his diminished vocal powers, we managed to communicate with each other quite satisfactorily. Our conversation ranged from the depressing atmosphere which dominated his surroundings to the gruff manner of the shepherd who cared for the sheep at Fernlysthwaite. My imitation of the big man's rudeness sent Con into a fit of laughter.

I admired the attractive, hand-knitted cardigan he was wearing and inquired if it had been made by his wife. Ignoring the reference to his wife, he explained that the garment had been one of a few Christmas presents given to him by June and Ted Picthall. June and Ted had moved away from our area two years previously. Their kindness to Con was maintained by correspondence, presents and twice yearly visits.

As I prepared to leave, I mentioned that it would be necessary for me to inform Mrs Brannigan of our forthcoming journey. Con's response which seemed especially delayed was, "I hope she won't make no trouble over it. But I'm going, any road, aren't I?"

Pretending a deal more confidence than I felt, I managed to convince him that all arrangements concerning the Lourdes pilgrimage were under control. With a solemn promise to keep him informed of future plans regarding his continental holiday, I left a more hopeful Con Brannigan in his little corner of the world.

A plump, jovial ward sister entertained me to the eternal tea and biscuit regime in her tiny office. She appeared to be very interested in the holiday scheme. The Catholic chaplain had mentioned the subject rather vaguely, some time ago. She felt that he had been making tentative inquiries into the reactions of the doctor in charge and herself. When she had told Father Brocklebank, earlier that afternoon, that they both agreed to his suggestion and felt that it was an excellent idea, he merely commented, "Good lass, I knew I could rely on you", leaving her in a state of ambiguity.

Sister had not mentioned to her staff that there was a possibility of one of their patients being whisked out of their midst to spend a week in France. She was overjoyed to learn that positive plans were already in motion which enabled her to impart the good tidings. She pledged her support stating that she and her ward staff would help in every way possible.

At that point in the conversation, I asked the pleasant lady if she would mind informing Mrs Brannigan about the affair next time she visited her husband. A frown clouded the cheerful face as the plump ward sister announced that Con's wife was rarely seen in the hospital. She felt that Mrs Brannigan treated her severely handicapped husband with great indifference. A few hours earlier, I would have shared those sentiments entirely, instead I found myself defending the woman now known to me as Hetty. I pointed out that Hillfoot Cottages were situated in a very isolated area, several miles from town and there was no regular bus service. Without further ado, I left Meadowlands Hospital and set out for Hillfoot.

The heavy iron ram's head resounded in its usual deafening manner. When Con's wife opened the door, she looked exactly the same as she had done on that first morning, three years previously. I approached her cautiously and sincerely hoped that she would not recognize me.

I inquired, "Mrs Brannigan, would it be possible to have a word with you, please?"

She beckoned me inside with her thumb, then pointed towards one of the rocking chairs at the side of the range. She sat on her usual seat by the sewing machine. She removed her funny little glasses from the end of her nose.

I began by saying that her husband had been chosen as one of the sick pilgrims to travel to Lourdes. She questioned me, "What do you mean by 'chosen'?" and "Who has chosen him?"

After a somewhat pregnant pause, I started with yet another question. "Do you know Father Brocklebank, Mrs Brannigan?"

She replied that she remembered a skinny, young lad from the village, down yonder, called Alfie Brocklebank. He had been sent off to one of them fancy schools when he was nowt but a li'le child that shouldn't have been separated from his mother.

She had not seen a great deal of him over the years. Any road, what had Alfie Brocklebank got to do with all this nonsense? I explained that he was prepared to pay her husband's expenses in an attempt to give Con at least one week out of 52 away from that miserable corner in Meadowlands. Father Brocklebank was also sponsoring a qualified nurse to take care of Con all the way to Lourdes and back.

She removed a handkerchief from the sleeve of her cardigan, blew her nose vigorously, replaced her handkerchief, then told me that she considered the whole business to be a ridiculous waste of time and money. The good Lord had never played any part in 'his' life; 'he' had never entered a church not even on 'his' wedding day. This oddly matched couple never referred to each other by anything other than 'he' and 'she' and 'him' and 'her'.

I answered, "Yes, Mrs Brannigan"; and that was recognition time. She peered at me in the dim light of her living room, then replaced her spectacles on the end of her nose, peered a little closer in my direction.

She inquired, "Are you the nurse what used to come and see to him?"

My reply, "Yes, Mrs Brannigan", was almost inaudible as I prepared to get out of the house as quickly as possible.

She accompanied me to the door. Instead of slamming it loudly and speedily, she remained standing while I unlocked my car, got inside and switched on the lights and ignition. The roadside at Hillfoot seemed to be darker and more lonesome than ever. As I was ready to release the handbrake, there was a knock on the passenger side window. Hetty Brannigan's face was pressed against it.

I switched off the engine, then stood on the deserted roadside, the car between us. My reaction was one of shock when Mrs Brannigan inquired, "Would you like a warm drink before you set off?"

When I had recovered sufficiently to decline her offer graciously, she said in a rather quiet tone, so far removed from her customary resonance, "Thanks lass for trying. Will you please thank Alfie Brocklebank for me? Who knows, happen some good will come out of it."

She actually smiled when she concluded her grateful speech. With a solemn promise to keep in contact with her during our preparations for the forthcoming trip abroad, I drove away from Hetty's isolated cottage.

Making my way home through the dark, deserted lanes and villages, I could not help wondering if the little shepherdess and her Lady of Lourdes were already using their mystical powers to influence this bizarre situation.

Chapter 6

The journey

The weeks immediately preceding our departure to Lourdes were filled with activity and fraught with a series of difficulties and frustrations.

The first problem arose when I agreed to accept responsibility for obtaining Con's passport. A kind photographer had gone along to Meadowlands Hospital, taken the necessary photographs and refused to accept a fee for his services. The helpful ward sister had managed to complete the required form. By holding a pen in Con's powerless right hand, she had procured a reasonably legible signature. An efficient resident doctor had signed his name and qualifications on the back of the photographs, testifying that they were a true likeness of the applicant. He had also written a letter which detailed the extent of the applicant's helplessness.

In spite of all efforts involved, the officer in charge of our local passport office insisted that the candidate applying for this important document must present himself in person, otherwise no passport could be issued. My suggestion that either he or one of his colleagues should visit Meadowlands Hospital and satisfy themselves that Cornelius Brendan Aloysius Brannigan did exist, met with a very haughty response. He certainly left me in no doubt whatsoever that I had insulted his prestige gravely.

Father Brocklebank solved the problem by contacting a rather distinguished gentleman who lived in our area. This chivalrous character compiled a lengthy and graphic account of the applicant and stated that he had known Mr Brannigan for many years. In actual fact, he had never seen the unfortunate Con. His epistle worked like a charm on the official and the passport was issued without any further ado.

Our next setback came in the form of the little shepherd developing a chest infection and for a while it looked very doubtful that he would be fit to travel. With the aid of antibiotic therapy and the hard work of the ward staff, the infection cleared quite quickly. Everyone heaved a mighty sigh of relief when the doctor in charge declared that all was well.

What looked like the final blow arrived with the delivery of the flight tickets. The aircraft detailed to convey the most seriously disabled pilgrims was due to take off from Blackpool airport at 7.30 am. We lived approximately 100 miles from the airport. There seemed no alternative means of getting there on time, other than driving through small hours, which would have proved too exhausting for Con.

This dilemma, however, was overcome by the highly organized team in charge of the diocesan pilgrimage. A telephone call from a doctor in the Blackpool area, who accepted responsibility for the travelling sick each year, informed me that patients in Mr Brannigan's category should be taken to Blackpool the day before departure. These very incapacitated pilgrims would be accommodated in a private nursing home under the patronage of the La Sagesse order of nuns.

The nursing home was sited close to the airport.

The sisters had an arrangement with their local branch of the Knights of Malta and Saint John's Ambulance Brigade. These two voluntary organizations provided transport for the sick pilgrims from the nursing home to the airport. The courteous voice on the other end of the telephone line expressed gratitude for my offer to nurse the sick at Lourdes and for my management of Mr Brannigan.

In a relieved and somewhat exultant mood, I decided to arrange the necessary transport from Meadowlands Hospital to the nursing home in Blackpool only to be confronted with yet another obstacle.

Our local ambulance controller stated the vehicles under his jurisdiction could only be used for purposes directly under the auspices of the National Health Service. As the Lourdes pilgrimage was very much a private affair, it would be impossible to authorize an ambulance to travel all those miles at least not without a charge. Following some calculations, he quoted the sum of £35 as the necessary cost to convey Con Brannigan and myself to and from Blackpool.

While appreciating the controller's point of view on the issue, I was compelled to decline his offer of making a provisional reservation, in the hope of finding alternative means of travel. Apart from a fairy godmother waving a magic wand over my mini and converting it into a vehicle large enough to accommodate a six foot stretcher, I could not conceive how this latest hurdle could be overcome. £35 amounted to a fortune to the majority of us in 1962.

The reverend and versatile Alfred Brocklebank, who tended to maintain a low profile in the frustrating preparations, unless he received an urgent plea from me, came to the rescue once again. He decided to use the parish dormobile that was normally used by the Boy Scouts for their regular outings. It was neither a safe nor comfortable conveyance. The interior which had been converted for our special occasion was covered in damp sand, sticky toffee papers, used lollipop sticks and the like, obviously a residue from the scouts last weekend at the seaside.

Con was dressed in a black suit provided by his benevolent hospital chaplain. Neither my heavy melton cloth district nursing coat nor his ill-fitting jacket and trousers could have been regarded as suitable attire for the rather hot and sunny day. We sweltered inside the cramped and dirty dormobile.

In addition to these disadvantages, Father Brocklebank was acting chauffeur. He drove with a seeming disregard for all other road users. As we sped down the motorway, a paralyzed man stretched out in the back of the odd vehicle, a district nurse holding him in a vice-like grip to prevent him toppling on to the floor and a reckless cleric at the wheel – we must have been the most peculiar combination ever to travel along the M6. I think it is quite true to say that the first stage of my first pilgrimage to Lourdes was an absolute nightmare. On reaching my destination, I felt that my four limbs were almost as useless as those of my travelling companion.

Inside the pleasant nursing home, however, all thoughts of previous discomfort were quickly dispelled. An atmosphere of peace, with no undue odour of sanctity prevailed. Nuns and lay nurses went about their daily business, carrying out their nursing duties exactly like their hospital counterparts. The only visible difference was that their

A shepherd getting sheep into the fold. Wigton, Cumbria.

A house on Kirby Moors, Cumbria.

Statue of St Bernadette

Bernadette Soubirous (1861)

"Que soy era Immaculada Councepciou"
"I am the Immaculate Conception"

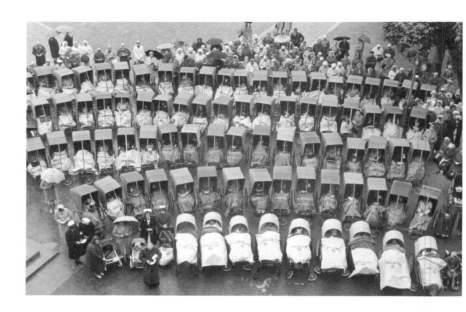

1972 Lancaster pilgrimage assembled in Rosary Square

A souvenir photo. The sick are always numerous.

Procession of the Blessed Sacrament and blessing of the sick

The Grotto – where pilgrims experience a peaceful presence

The fountains. "Go and drink from the spring and wash yourself there."

"Go and tell the priest to build a chapel here
and to have people come in procession."

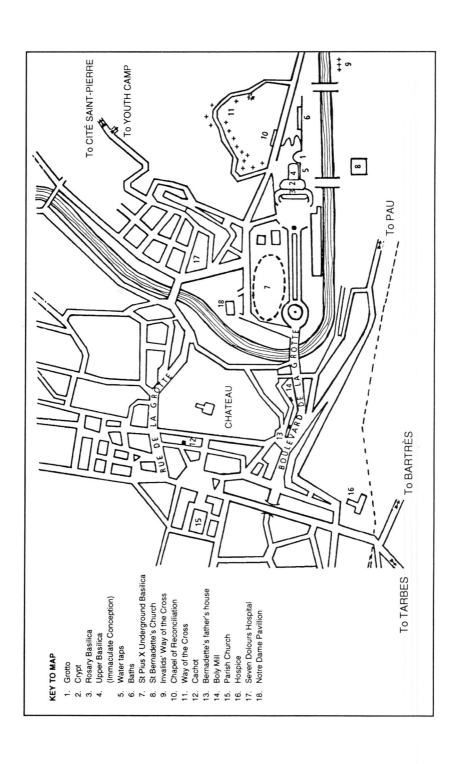

KEY TO MAP

1. Grotto
2. Crypt
3. Rosary Basilica
4. Upper Basilica
   (Immaculate Conception)
5. Water taps
6. Baths
7. St Pius X Underground Basilica
8. St Bernadette's Church
9. Invalids' Way of the Cross
10. Chapel of Reconciliation
11. Way of the Cross
12. Cachot
13. Bernadette's father's house
14. Boly Mill
15. Parish Church
16. Hospice
17. Seven Dolours Hospital
18. Notre Dame Pavillion

To CITÉ SAINT-PIERRE

To YOUTH CAMP

To PAU

To BARTRÈS

To TARBES

CHATEAU

RUE DE LA GROTTE

BOULEVARD DE LA GROTTE

patients were tucked away in private rooms behind closed doors.

Tea was served in a comfortably furnished lounge. It was during that welcome respite I learned that several of the staff were to accompany us on the next part of our journey. It was a policy of this order to supply nursing staff for the travelling sick each year. Because of the number of sick pilgrims from outlying areas being housed in the home overnight, it was necessary for me to book into a hotel.

A pretty-faced nun with a broken English accent performed this chore for me by telephone. Afterwards she escorted me along a quiet corridor, with closed doors on either side, to say farewell to my patient. Con was lying in bed between snow white sheets in a deeply carpeted room which was equipped with every modern convenience. He seemed a world away from the barn in Fernlysthwaite where he had spent so many nights in the past.

Next morning, shortly after half past six, I joined forces with my fellow volunteers and the other sick pilgrims at Blackpool air terminal. The matron in charge of the pilgrimage had forwarded the necessary instructions some weeks earlier. Among the rules and regulations was a polite request from the lady to wear uniform according to status as far as possible. This request was made in an attempt to assist her to issue orders accordingly to nursing personnel who were unknown to her.

This seemed like a mammoth, if not impossible, task. However, during that first week I spent in Lourdes, I learned that this slender dark-haired girl with her gentle manner, quiet voice and sweet smile organized this very mixed band of nursing volunteers with a cool efficiency that might well have forced many experienced hospital matrons twice her age to hang their heads in humiliation. She ranked as a midwifery sister in her place of employment and had been travelling to Lourdes with the sick pilgrims since her student days. Four years previously, she had been elected by the diocesan pilgrimage committee to assume overall control of the nursing side of the venture. It was certainly difficult to imagine anyone more suited to the role.

In addition to our directions, each volunteer received a register listing the 126 people who would be in our care from the moment we assembled at Blackpool airport until our return. This informative document catalogued our charges in detail: name, address, age, diagnosis, treatments and the extent of his or her disability.

Two large aeroplanes could be seen on the runway. The reception area was crammed with men, women and children. Many of these people, due to some incapacity or other were confined to wheelchairs. Brandcardiers (stretcher bearers) were already hard at work, arranging these chairbound people and their luggage in an orderly queue ready for passport inspection.

Brandcardiers are a fraternity of extraordinary gentlemen from many different walks of life, of various nationalities and age groups. They sacrifice part of their holidays each year in order to convey stretcher-bound patients, not only during their stay in Lourdes but also en route. Stretcher bearing entails a deal of extremely hard work and a considerable lack of sleep because of the very early morning preparations which are part of their duties.

Brandcardiers can be easily recognized during the pilgrimages by the characteristic straps which they wear round their shoulders. In spite of the wide variations in ages, temperaments, professions and nationalities they work together in perfect harmony with one specific aim in view – to get the sick pilgrims to Lourdes and home again safely. They also transport them to different venues of worship during their stay.

French brandcardiers control the main flow of invalid traffic during religious services. They form part of the Hospitalité de Notre Dame, a voluntary organization that operates in the small town through-out the peak periods which begin in April and end in September.

Women attired in bright blue nylon overalls and matching head dresses predominated the scene within the air terminal. These blue clad ladies like to be known as the Lourdes handmaids. Like the brandcardiers, they come from different walks of life to assist in the domestic arrangements of the pilgrim-age. Handmaids are an extremely important section of the work force.

Mainly their duties revolve round the serving of meals and the feeding of helpless patients. They also do their fair share of conveying the sick pilgrims to and from various points within the religious domain. These ladies, generally, make it a rule to transport an adequate sufficiency of English food. They can always be relied upon to produce that dearly longed for cup of tea in the predominantly coffee-drinking country.

Nurses in all shades of uniform hovered around. Few of us were known to each other as the Lancaster diocese extends from Carlisle in Cumbria to Fleetwood in Lancashire. Preston and its surround-ing areas had produced the largest contingent of nursing staff. Many of them had served on previous pilgrimages and their helpful comments were greatly appreciated by the newcomers.

Formal introductions would have been impossible in such a situation and indeed, were unnecessary as everyone worked, laughed and generally enjoyed the experience. We spent a lot of time searching suitcases, handbags and different other items of luggage for passports that our new-found patients had put 'in a safe place'.

Each sick person was issued with a broad, black, plastic arm band bearing a large red cross and the word 'LANCASTER' printed in sizable red letters. Each worker was given a similar emblem, the only visible difference being that these were made of white plastic material as opposed to the sick pilgrim's black.

These distinctive armlets proved to be of great significance when hundreds of invalids from many parts of Britain and several other countries were packed together on stretchers and in carriages participating in a religious service. On these occasions, nurses and brandcardiers with water flasks slung over their shoulders mingled and moved freely among them. The language barrier presented very few problems. When an invalid indicated that he or she required attention, a drink from the flask met with a nod of approval resulting in a satisfied customer without the use of words.

There were occasions, however, when something more than a drink was required. If patient and nurse were unable to communicate, the policy was to find a nurse wearing a corresponding armlet to that of the troubled patient. When the nurse arrived on the scene, it was advisable to remain close at hand, ready to render assistance should the invalid need to be removed from the assembly and returned to the hospital.

Our willing work force at Blackpool airport that first morning, was augmented by members of the Knights of Malta and Saint John's Ambulance Brigade. When the six stretcher cases arrived, each one accompanied by a sister of the La Sagesse community, they were, of course, given priority. Con Brannigan was the occupant of the third stretcher. I observed his departure from a short distance and noticed that his white veiled escort held two passports in her hand. Neither she nor Con would ever know the difficulty and the ultimate deceit involved in obtaining the small navy blue document. She carried my overnight bag that contained the few articles of clothing that I had begged and borrowed for the helpless little shepherd, whose face, at that point in time, was wreathed in smiles.

Accommodating these severely disabled persons inside the aircraft proved to be a lengthy procedure. It was essential for each wooden stretcher to be secured to the floor with strong ropes. Three such pilgrims travelled on each plane.

Wheelchair-bound pilgrims were the next batch to be presented at the passport inspection desk. As each volunteer wheeled the patient forward, he or she presented their own passport and that of the sick person. From there it was but a few yards to the flight desk. Once relieved of our baggage, we were able to set off at a much brisker pace through the flight gates and across the tarmac towards the waiting planes.

Brandcardiers and the experienced male members of the Knights of Malta and Saint John's Ambulance Brigade carried those disabled people up the dangerously narrow gangways into the aircraft with what could best be described as amazing grace. Once inside, these invalids were placed in their seats and secured with the standard safety belts. Wheelchairs were folded and packed in the hold by the airport staff.

The walking sick formed the last part of our disabled travellers. Some of them walked awkwardly and with great difficulty. Many could manage to inch along with the aid of clumsy calipers, while others struggled bravely, leaning heavily on crutches or sticks.

One doctor, several nurses, handmaids and brandcardiers travelled on each of the invalid planes. Many other volunteers followed on later flights. Healthy pilgrims, relatives and friends of the travelling sick and quite a few clerical gentlemen followed on these later flights.

Our very mixed bunch of passengers soon settled and became quite a lively party as they were led in song, terribly off key, by one of the handmaids. 'She's my lassie from Lancashire' and many more well known ditties rang out as we were piloted towards France.

Work commenced with the serving of breakfast. As several of our participants were severely handicapped, it was necessary to spoon-feed them. Helping with this feeding procedure enabled me to become acquainted with some of my travelling companions.

Firstly, there was the young mother seated between her 10-year-old son and pretty, blonde, 8-year-old daughter, both of whom suffered from cerebral palsy. Attempting to feed the 10-year-old spastic boy whose swallowing mechanism was so severely impaired proved to be an almost impossible task at first. However, following a few helpful hints from his wonderful mother, I managed to transfer the porridge from the plastic container to the boy's stomach quite successfully.

I learned from the mother whose son and daughter had been so grossly short-changed by fate, that she had two younger children who were quite healthy. For that she was thankful. How could one help but marvel at her courage in embarking on two further pregnancies and her efficient management of her two spastic youngsters? I looked into the hazel eyes of the tubby, little redhead for some sign of resentment or pity. There was none. She answered my searching gaze by saying,

"My husband and myself have been given great strength and numerous blessings that compensate for what many of our friends refer to as our double tragedy."

There was the 28-year-old dark-haired and emaciated gentleman, dressed impeccably in a navy blue lounge suit and dazzling white shirt. He was struggling to feed himself. His severe lack of energy due to his advanced state of leukaemia was making this simple, natural exercise appear as a real laborious task. He declined my offer to help, with a wan smile, explaining that he preferred to eat his food slowly.

Passing down the aircraft, I noticed our young matron dealing with a middle-aged woman whose main complaint was her intense fear of flying. She insisted on shouting,

"Please, please tell the driver to stop. I want to go home."

That particular female caused a great deal of anxiety and hard work on the outward journey.

As the plane passed over the Channel Islands, some well-meaning individual suggested that she look out of the window and admire the islands glistening like diamonds in the sunlight. That proposal proved to be a grave error of judgement on the part of the benefactor. As the hysterical lady looked downwards she screamed loudly, struggled to get out of her seat then fainted, as the young matron, a doctor and a charming air hostess were doing their utmost to reassure and comfort her.

Her recovery from the attack of syncopae was immediately followed by a bout of vomiting. Soon her stomach contents were spilling down not only her own clothing but that of the three good Samaritans. As it was impossible to procure changes of clothing, there followed the tedious and unpleasant chore of cleaning all garments with small quantities of water supplied in plastic containers from the serving area, by a second helpful air hostess.

I made my way to the rear of the plane where three stretcher cases were firmly secured to the floor. Con Brannigan was not one of them. He was already well ahead in the preceding aircraft. I knelt on the floor and began a conversation with a pleasant young woman who informed me that she had been employed as a health visitor until two years previously when she suffered a brain tumour.

Neuro-surgery had relieved her of the tumour. Unfortunately she had a residual paraplegia. Her urinary incontinence had been overcome by the insertion of a self-retaining catheter. The tragic girl, like the mother of the two spastic children, emphasized her gratitude to God for preserving her sanity, as so many of her fellow sufferers were left with a gross intellectual deficit.

She was just one more example of the outstanding stoicism that was being manifested among this exceptional collection of sick people. Her main concern, at that particular point in time, was fear of food spilling on her rather lovely pink outfit. It was in the company of this remarkable person that I spent the greater part of my journey to France.

We shared a common interest in that our normal nursing lives were involved in the community and not inside hospital walls. There were plenty of experiences to exchange and the cheerful girl's quips and anecdotes soon diverted my thoughts from her disability. When she requested me to move her legs into a more comfortable position, the reality of the situation was abruptly brought home to me. It was a most disquieting experience to acknowledge the realism of the catastrophic situation; which was simply that unless a miraculous cure was achieved through faith healing, the attractive brunette was destined to spend the remainder of her life confined to a spinal carriage. Her affliction was crippling and humiliating.

It was in this strange, but not at all unhappy, atmosphere that we prepared for touchdown at Tarbes airport. The spiritual purpose of our journey was indicated to us by the chaplain to the sick pilgrims. He led us into the recitation of the rosary which was followed by singing the Lourdes hymn, 'Ave, Ave, Ave Maria...'. This swinging air is heard constantly in the strange town. Clocks on public buildings play it every quarter of an hour, musical boxes in souvenir shops give their tinny rendering of it over and over again. From early morning until long after dark, choirs of various nationalities sing it loudly in their native tongues.

Our sick pilgrims were unloaded at Tarbes with the assistance of members of the Hospitalité de Notre Dame. Our troublesome female patient found herself being lifted from her seat by a youthful French brandcardier who asked her in his attractive, faltering English accent why she looked so worried. When she replied tearfully that she wanted to go home, the humorous young Frenchman adjusted his beret and gave the obese lady a resounding kiss. As he carried her off the plane, he announced, to everyone's amusement, in a feigned peevish tone,

"Ah, Madame, you disappoint me very much. I thought you had travelled all those miles just to be in my arms."

He planted another kiss on her sweaty and tear-stained cheek, then carried on a conversation, in his native tongue, with one of his associates who was engaged in getting our handsome leukaemia sufferer off the plane.

Our helpful young stranger supported the rather weighty lady in his youthful arms all the way to one of the waiting coaches, where two nurses from the Cumbrian area were engaged with seating arrangements. One of them inquired in her pronounced Cumbrian dialect which was similar to the troublesome patient's,

"Ee, Elsie, have you got summat up with your legs, then? Get yourself down this minute, before you do that li'le lad a mischief."

Scrutiny of Elsie's dossier revealed that she did not suffer any physical disorder whatsoever. She was, in fact a very agile schizophrenic with a remarkable aptitude for climbing over walls and fences and moving with great alacrity from various institutions that had housed her.

Officials at Tarbes are so accustomed to invalid planes arriving on their airport that they have given a deal of consideration to clearance. An enormous amount of time is saved and inconvenience averted by their method of inspecting passport within the aircraft. Naturally, this routine is used only when the occupants are as severely incapacitated as ours were on that morning in May 1962.

Coaches specifically designed for the transportation of disabled persons were used to and from Tarbes airport. Each of these vehicles had in its ceiling area four extended luggage rack devices. Each one of these contraptions could accommodate a stretcher case. Approximately 46 pilgrims complemented our seating capacity within the coach.

Luggage was carried in the conventional manner which is a compartment on the outside rear of the vehicle. There have seldom been hitches recorded concerning luggage deliveries in spite of the numerous assortments of cases, holdalls and the like. These seem to appear almost miraculously at the correct destination.

Volunteers are normally booked into hotels as close to the hospitals as possible. Again each volunteer's baggage appears in his or her bedroom as if by magic, so very efficient are the promoters of the pilgrimage.

The first leg of the journey from Helmsvale to Blackpool had been uncomfortable and frightening at times. However, the last part, from Tarbes to Lourdes was perilous and terrifying to say the least. A foolhardy French driver who appeared to relinquish caution completely continued to increase speed until it seemed that we were travelling along the rural road at a maximum velocity with only two wheels negotiating dangerous bends and corners.

Three of our stretchers were occupied by a trio of grossly incapacitated people. Four nurses, doing their utmost to maintain their own balance inside the speeding coach, swayed wildly as they tried desperately to keep some sort of hold on their helpless charges in the ceiling area. We were aware of the very frightening fact that we were utterly powerless to help should a mishap occur.

However, records show a complete absence of reference to accidents concerning handicapped people and their helpers who have travelled this route since Tarbes became the recognized airport for reception and departure of such pilgrims. Perhaps this is one more of the miracles that can be attributed to the supernatural influence that prevails in that unique corner of the world.

It was probably to keep in favour with divine providence that our chaplain decided on prayer as the only course available to us in such hazardous circumstances. Once again he led us in the rosary recital and during the singing of 'Ave, Ave, Ave Maria...'. Our coach driver, at last, reduced speed dramatically as he manoeuvred the vehicle most expertly through the very narrow and hilly streets of the world famous town in the foothills of the Pyrenees.

Disappointment and, indeed, disenchantment were my initial reactions to the place that emanated an atmosphere of the typical, cheap resort with its garish souvenir shops cluttering the crushed pavements with their colourful, astronomically priced and mostly useless miscellany. Masses of noisy people crowded round the tables outside the numer-

26th April 1992

Dear children I do love you infinitely! Don't be sad if your life is not filled with divine favours.

It is not this that is important. What is important is that you persevere in prayer and do not give in when life becomes hurtful. I am the Blessed Mother who shall come in the midst of all your misfortunes and keep you safe. You should know this! Be as good as you can. Live in faith all I tell you!"

Pray! Pray! Pray!

(Page 413, of Our Lady's Message of Mercy to the World.)

Information:

© Friends of the Mother of Divine Mercy
7 Somerset Close, Whitstable,
Kent CT5 4RA, England.

Nihil Obstat: Dublin 22 March 2000.
Rev. Jerome McCarthy D.D. Censor Dublin Diocese.

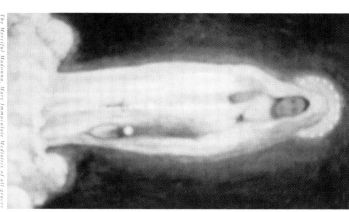

The Merciful Madonna, Mary Immaculate Mediatrix of all graces

"You who stand between Earth and Heaven save us"

THE MEANING OF THE IMAGE

"Today I am going to tell you the meaning of My Image and the seven showings contained in it."

1. The halo around My Head is the 12 stars.

2. There is a host of Cherubs in the form of a cloud at My Feet.

3. A Rosary of 15 Mysteries fall from My Hands joined in prayer.

4. My Garment is clothed with the Sun.

5. In the folds of My Left Arm Christ is crucified.

6. The left side of My Garment is covered in the Precious Blood, which falls from the Cross of My Son, forming a brown stain.

7. A Host is suspended over a Chalice beneath this brown stain.

"Let him who has eyes to see, see, and let him who has faith believe. I am the Mediatrix. This is the meaning of the image."

17th June 1998

Have this image printed with the inscription :-
"You who stand between Earth and Heaven save us."

OUR LADY'S MESSAGE   17th June 1998

"Dear Child, the exposure that has remained in your possession is a miraculous one and must be exposed and venerated. This one also, copies may be made for the faithful that it be honoured. Where it is honoured special graces, even astounding miracles may be obtained when blessed. Great graces will rain down on souls that carry this image on them while constantly remembering My Motherly love for each soul and repeating the prayer:-

Act of Reparation

Mary Immaculate † I beg of you † obtain pardon for me † and I ask through Your Immaculate. Heart † save us from sin † and lead all to Heaven. Amen.

(† indicates a pause)

21st January 1995

"As may times as you say this you will be saving a sinner."

16th May 1999

"...And let it be known that I desire also to grant special favours to souls that say this prayer before My Image while imploring My Mercy".

"Our Lady, Mediatrix of all Graces, be blessed on earth as You are in Heaven and may I take delight in Your company during my day and may You chase Satan away with Your glances, now and at the hour of my death. Amen"

THE MEANING OF THE IMAGE

"Today I am going to tell you the meaning of My Image and the seven showings contained in it."

1. The halo around My Head is the 12 stars.
2. There is a host of Cherubs in the form of a cloud at My Feet.
3. A Rosary of 15 Mysteries fall from My Hands joined in prayer.
4. My Garment is clothed with the Sun.
5. In the folds of My Left Arm Christ is crucified.
6. The left side of My Garment is covered in the Precious Blood, which falls from the Cross of My Son, forming a brown stain.
7. A Host is suspended over a Chalice beneath this brown stain.

"Let him who has eyes to see, see, and let him who has faith believe. I am the Mediatrix. This is the meaning of the image."

17ᵗʰ June 1998

Have this image printed with the inscription :-
"You who stand between Earth and Heaven save us."

OUR LADY'S MESSAGE   17ᵗʰ June 1998

"Dear Child, the exposure that has remained in your possession is a miraculous one and must be exposed and venerated. This one also, copies may be made for the faithful that it be honoured. Where it is honoured special graces, even astounding miracles may be obtained when blessed. Great graces will rain down on souls that carry this image on them while constantly remembering My Motherly love for each soul and repeating the prayer:-

Act of Reparation

Mary Immaculate † I beg of you † obtain pardon for me † and I ask through Your Immaculate. Heart † save us from sin † and lead all to Heaven. Amen.

(† indicates a pause)

21ˢᵗ January 1995

"As may times as you say this you will be saving a sinner."

16ᵗʰ May 1999

"...And let it be known that I desire also to grant special favours to souls that say this prayer before My Image while imploring My Mercy".

"Our Lady, Mediatrix of all Graces, be blessed on earth as You are in Heaven and may I take delight in Your company during my day and may You chase Satan away with Your glances, now and at the hour of my death. Amen"

17ᵗʰ June 1998

26th April 1992

Dear children I do love you infinitely! Don't be sad if your life is not filled with divine favours.

It is not this that is important. What is important is that you persevere in prayer and do not give in when life becomes hurtful. I am the Blessed Mother who shall come in the midst of all your misfortunes and keep you safe. You should know this! Be as good as you can. Live in faith all I tell you!"

Pray! Pray! Pray!

(Page 413, of Our Lady's Message of Mercy to the World.)

Information:

© Friends of the Mother of Divine Mercy
7 Somerset Close, Whitstable,
Kent CT5 4RA, England.

Nihil Obstat: Dublin 22 March 2000.
Rev. Jerome McCarthy D.D. Censor Dublin Diocese.

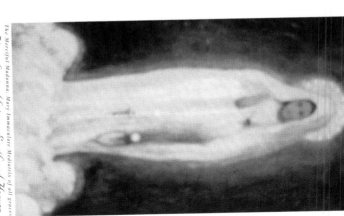

The Merciful Madonna. Mary Immaculate Mediatrix of all graces
"You also stand between Earth and Heaven save us"

OUR LADY'S MESSAGE
17th June 1998

"Dear Child, the exposure that has remained in your possession is a miraculous one and must be exposed and venerated. This one also, copies may be made for the faithful that it be honoured. Where it is honoured special graces, even astounding miracles may be obtained when blessed. Great graces will rain down on souls that carry this image on them while constantly remembering My Motherly love for each soul and repeating the prayer:-

Act of Reparation

Mary Immaculate † I beg of you † obtain pardon for me † and I ask through Your Immaculate. Heart † save us from sin † and lead all to Heaven. Amen.

(† indicates a pause)

21st January 1995

"As may times as you say this you will be saving a sinner."

16th May 1999

"...And let it be known that I desire also to grant special favours to souls that say this prayer before My Image while imploring My Mercy".

"Our Lady, Mediatrix of all Graces, be blessed on earth as You are in Heaven and may I take delight in Your company during my day and may You chase Satan away with Your glances, now and at the hour of my death. Amen"

THE MEANING OF THE IMAGE
(13th July 1995)

"Today I am going to tell you the meaning of My Image and the seven showings contained in it."

1. The halo around My Head is the 12 stars.
2. There is a host of Cherubs in the form of a cloud at My Feet.
3. A Rosary of 15 Mysteries fall from My Hands joined in prayer.
4. My Garment is clothed with the Sun.
5. In the folds of My Left Arm Christ is crucified.
6. The left side of My Garment is covered in the Precious Blood, which falls from the Cross of My Son, forming a brown stain.
7. A Host is suspended over a Chalice beneath this brown stain.

"Let him who has eyes to see, see, and let him who has faith believe. I am the Mediatrix. This is the meaning of the image."

17th June 1998

Have this image printed with the inscription :-
"You who stand between Earth and Heaven save us."

26th April 1992

Dear children I do love you infinitely! Don't be sad if your life is not filled with divine favours.

It is not this that is important. What is important is that you persevere in prayer and do not give in when life becomes hurtful. I am the Blessed Mother who shall come in the midst of all your misfortunes and keep you safe. You should know this! Be as good as you can. Live in faith all I tell you!"

Pray! Pray! Pray!

(Page 413, of Our Lady's Message of Mercy to the World.)

Information:

© Friends of the Mother of Divine Mercy
7 Somerset Close, Whitstable,
Kent CT5 4RA, England.

Nihil Obstat: Dublin 22 March 2000.
Rev. Jerome McCarthy D.D. Censor Dublin Diocese.

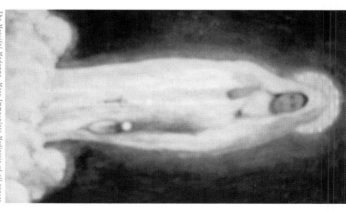

The Merciful Madonna, Mary Immaculate Mediatrix of all graces

"You also stand between Earth and Heaven save us"

ous cafés voraciously consuming coffee and beer.

This scene, however, quickly changed to one of peace, serenity and reverence as we passed through Saint Joseph's Gate into the domain Massabielle. The throngs of people who milled around the confines of the domain spoke in almost whispered tones. Small groups huddled together reciting the rosary in hushed voices. A male Italian voice resounded through a microphone as he preached to his people on the virtues of Bernadette Soubirous.

Thankfully, beds were already prepared to receive our weary travelling sick pilgrims, inside the Accueil de Notre Dame Hospital. The Accueil de Notre Dame was the largest hospital in Lourdes at that time. Most severely handicapped persons were allocated to wards on the ground floor. Less severely afflicted people were taken by lift to the second and third floors.

Through this method of bed allocation, I discovered a phenomenal means of communication existed among those grossly stricken human beings. Two large wards on ground floor level housed approximately 60 such persons; men being accommodated in one ward and women in the other. Utility rooms separated the two.

Those sorely afflicted men and women had journeyed to those wards from many countries, such as Britain, Ireland, Belgium, Italy, Spain, Holland, Germany and many parts of France. Their native languages were unknown to one another. The peculiar bond that existed among them, however, enabled them to overcome the language barrier completely. It became quite usual, while working among them, to witness the exchange of tit-bits, the interested and pleased expressions on their faces, as they looked at each other's family photographs. Somehow they seemed to be able to relate to each other quite satisfactorily. How often I have wished that those among us who are blessed with normal faculties and health, would behave towards each other and try to understand each other's points of view in a similar manner to those unfortunate men and women who occupied the beds in the Accueil de Notre Dame Hospital.

With our patients safely ensconced in their new abode, a midday meal was served accompanied by the now familiar feeding procedure. It was during the lunch period that I made my first contact with Con Brannigan since we had said our farewells in the luxurious nursing home almost 24 hours previously.

As I sat on the side of his bed, he managed between mouthfuls of food to tell me how much he was enjoying himself. He requested me to remove a purse from his jacket pocket, take the money from it and buy 'a bit of something for 'her and the lads'. The little, black leather purse bore the Meadowlands Hospital ward sister's initials. It contained £12 which had been collected by her and the caring staff of the geriatric ward.

When our patients had been settled down for a well-deserved rest, volunteers went along to their hotels. When they had officially booked into their rooms and had a meal, they returned to the hospital to work with the sick pilgrims until the arrival of our night staff at 8.30.

As I sank into bed that night, thoroughly exhausted, my feelings concerning the Lourdes pilgrimage were very confused. Certainly, I never imagined that it was to be the first of many nights that I was to spend in that strange town.

Chapter 7

The people and places of Lourdes

Built on part of the River Gave de Pau, the rather unlovely little town of Lourdes is probably one of the most famous and popular places in the world. Every year, its resident population of approximately 20,300 receives between 5 and 6 million visitors. The millions of people who throng into its narrow streets do not arrive just as tourists or holiday makers – they go there for many different reasons.

Primarily, there are the sick pilgrims. Some of them may well be hoping for a miraculous cure of his or her individual affliction. Bernadette Soubirous has never been recorded as stating that her Aquero promised miraculous cures at the grotto Massabielle. Others among that category may be praying for the courage and strength to accept or come to terms with the adversity that besets them. Then, there are the voluntary workers who accompany the sick people and tend to their manifold needs.

Thirdly, there are the relatives and friends of the sick pilgrims who feel obliged to make the journey with their incapacitated loved ones. A fourth group consists of perfectly healthy human beings, who for their own personal reasons choose to visit Lourdes rather than an exotic or ostentatious holiday resort.

Lourdes is fundamentally the city of the sick. They form the nucleus and are given priority over everyone else. In the midst of the heavy traffic congestion and confusion in the narrow streets, all vehicles cede to the long lines of invalid carriages and the clumsy, calipered, lower limbs of the cripples inching bravely along from one point to another.

In spite of this pre-eminence, voluntary workers must never lose sight of the fact that the handicapped people are autonomous Christians. It is easy to come to regard them as praying objects that are conveyed from one venue of worship to another.

During the last 25 years, the modern one-day pilgrims have become so increasingly popular that a special service has been established to meet their needs. This type of visitor consists mainly of people who are holidaying in the vicinity. There are also those who have travelled many miles to avail themselves of a hasty look at the strange town. In some instances, it may well be curiosity that is the impelling force behind these sojourners.

Clerics speaking different languages are at their disposition to advise on daily programmes. The latest church to be built and opened in 1988, Saint Bernadette's, situated in the field opposite the grotto Massabielle, has within its spacious confines a special Day Pilgrim Centre.

Young people are very much in evidence and form a prominent part of the voluntary work force of each contingency from every country. It is an extremely encouraging experience to behold these teenage boys and girls toiling so hard from dawn until the hours of darkness. They convey the sick pilgrims hither and thither, helping them in every way possible. Their youthful cheerfulness often reflecting in the smiling faces of the stretcher borne invalids. Their abundant energy extends far into the night hours. Long after older pilgrims have retired, crowds of these remarkable youngsters assemble in the streets to play their guitars and give their own special renderings of spiritual refrains in diverse tongues and with unbounded enthusiasm.

There are also the typical teenagers of this day and age: the products of our modern society, who arrive in Lourdes without the support of an organized pilgrimage. They arrive on bicycles, motorbikes and on foot, some of them having hitched-hiked many miles. A large number of them may hold view points and moral standards contrary to those shared by the majority of Lourdes visitors. It is not unusual for this type of young person to declare openly that he or she is completely without religious convictions. Their presence in the unique town demonstrates beyond doubt that these casual travellers are searching for something. The first thing they discover is a warm welcome with the offer of food and shelter and an invitation to the Rotonde which is the meeting place for all youth in Lourdes. It is situated in the large field facing the grotto Massabielle. A youth camp consisting of tents and some brick buildings under the auspices of a highly organized youth council is open for most months of the pilgrimage season.

During the youthful gatherings, participants are encouraged to join in the various discussions, to express their opinions and problems and to unite in prayer, singing and guitar playing. In such a relaxed atmosphere, friendship, respect and understanding are generated. Consequently the Rotonde becomes a starting point for a great many of these casual young folk. They leave the grotto Massabielle with a deeper comprehension of life and the countless difficulties it presents. Quite a number of them return to the Lourdes scene to augment the voluntary work force.

Amid the opulence and extravagance of the narrow streets where money passes across the counters of the souvenir shops, cafés and bars almost incessantly, the familiar text, 'For you have the poor among you always' (Jn 12:6) can be easily disregarded. Yet, only 15 minutes walk away from the affluent environment, sited obtrusively in 14 acres of grassland is the peaceful Cité Saint-Pierre. Cité Saint-Pierre functions solely as a haven for those people who cherish a desire to visit Lourdes, but cannot afford the costs involved in an arranged pilgrimage.

Its diminutive chapel built of stone and teak with its tiny windows is in total contrast to the splendid, ornamental architectural masterpieces associated with Lourdes. On the surface of the uneven, flagged floor are a couple of dozen backless stools, each loosely covered with a faded sheepskin. These stools are the only items of furniture contained in the dark, austere and unique venue of worship.

Cité Saint-Pierre previously known as Cité Secours or City of the Poor was founded in 1876 and a shelter close to the grotto Massabielle was used to house the visiting poor. The shelter was demolished to make way for the construction of the esplanade. It was not until 1 May 1965 that Cité Saint-Pierre was officially opened.

The main feature of the esplanade is Rosary Square, which can hold 100,000 people. Here stands a stately statue of the Virgin Mary, which faces the unique triple church arrangement of three structures built directly underneath each other – the upper Basilica of the Immaculate Conception was the first to be built. The gigantic Rosary Basilica designed by leopold

Hardy was the second building. Wedged between is the crypt of the original which was where Bernadette attended Mass ad the consecration ceremony.

Then, of course, there is the grotto Massabielle itself. The world famous grotto, which is the very essence of Lourdes, is beautiful in its simplicity. Everything within the domain has been changed dramatically from the garbage dump of Bernadette's day to the grandeur and splendour of today. Yet, the grotto has remained unspoiled. A slab hewn from the grey rock forms the humble altar, which is sited at the entrance to the cave. From behind the cave runs the spring, flowing at the rate of 27,000 gallons a day. This water is stored in a reservoir underneath the Rosary basilica, then diverted to the water taps and the baths.

In a niche in the rock face, high above the altar and surrounded by a rose bush, stands a simple marble statue of the Virgin Mary. Inscribed on the pedestal are the words in patois dialect 'Que soy era Immaculada Councepciou'. In the huge candelabra, immediately outside the entrance to the grotto, candles burn constantly. Local people keep them alight when the pilgrimage season is finished.

The shallow cavern contains one wooden bench, therefore seating accommodation within it is restricted to approximately five or six people. Several wooden benches placed on the pavement, in front of the simple grotto, are always packed with pilgrims. Many more kneel or stand on the esplanade, regardless of the very heavy rainfalls peculiar to that part of the world. They kneel or stand and pray privately. Some form little groups and offer their prayers quietly in their own vernacular. Praying at the grotto is a 24 hour a day ritual, though the number of pilgrims decreases considerably during the night hours.

Special overnight vigils are, however, quite popular and many of us adherents travel to Lourdes specifically for this devotion. For it is at night, with only the sound of the river rippling past and the flickering and occasional splutter of the burning candles, that this lowly cave must certainly be the closest concept of heaven that earthly people could possibly imagine. Its magnetic effect on those of us who keep going there year after year is utterly impossible to describe in words.

Chapter 8
Caring for the travelling sick

Sprawling along the far right side of Rosary Square, surrounded by trees and shrubs, is the grey stone-built Accueil de Notre Dame, the popular hospital, known to all English speaking people as the 'Asile'. The Asile has 40 rooms and normally houses 720 sick travellers.

The hospital has had several annexes and extensions added to it throughout the years. It is a sort of rare combination of ancient and modern building patterns and therefore looks like a bizarre compound ranging from the sublime to the ridiculous.

The wide foyer of the hospital with its brown walls and cold, mosaic floor is chilling and uninviting when empty. This chilling influence is, however, overcome by the masses of people who gather within it several times during the day.

The foyer is the mustering centre of the sick pilgrims who occupy the beds of this strange building. It is here that human beings suffering from every abnormal condition imaginable, and stricken with the most grotesque deformities can be seen.

The extra long wards are furnished with the old fashioned black iron bedsteads. Due to overwhelming numbers of sick pilgrims, these beds are usually arranged much closer together than the standard space stipulated by hospital authorities. Each patient's belongings are accommodated in a large rack attached underneath the bed.

Several single and double rooms lead off the main wards. These are usually reserved for sick clergy, members of religious orders and extremely ill lay pilgrims.

Clinical rooms are large and airy, compared with the ward situation. These are shared by different visiting medical and nursing personnel. It is not, therefore, unusual while performing surgical dressings or preparing injections to find oneself in the company of nurses from other countries. They carry out similar procedures and treatments and converse with their patients in their native language.

The Asile, despite its depressing exterior, formidable foyer, cramped conditions and inadequate hygiene facilities, has without a shadow of a doubt the most friendly atmosphere in the world. There exists a profound sense of comradeship within its walls. This camaraderie breaks down all barriers and it is inside this strange, French hospital that nurses and doctors, with the aid of sign language, an occasional phrase book and a lot of smiles, work together in perfect harmony helping each other to help the helpless.

The concrete ramps leading down to the subterranean basilica of Pius X are located fairly close to the rear of the Asile, thus providing easy access for stretchers and invalid carriages, to and from that venue of worship.

The Seven Dolours Hospital is sited outside the domain, at the far end of the Avenue de Bernadette Soubirous. It is capable of accommodating 550 sick pilgrims. It has a large reception centre which is particularly useful for the assembly of stretchers and invalid carriages. Because of the location of the Seven Dolours Hospital, strenuous effort is involved in transporting the sick pilgrims to and from the domain.

One of the most recent buildings to be erected in the prairie is the Accueil de Saint Bernadette. This modern hospital was opened in 1977. Unlike its aged counterparts, it is roomy, more generous with bed space and, therefore, feels a lot less claustrophobic. Toilet and washing facilities, unlike the other two hospitals, are consistent with the hygienic standards of today. This latest hospital can house between 500 and 600 sick pilgrims. A pleasant, airy and light chapel is situated conveniently in the main entrance area.

For the efficient day to day management of these hospitals, in addition to nuns, nurses and brandcardiers, who accompany the sick travellers, there is a voluntary work force of 50 to 100 people, varying in age from 18 to 70 years. They come from all walks of life to look after the welfare of the sick people. They help with the laundry, ironing, washing up and general cleaning. There are also lay nurses among this voluntary work force. These volunteers belong to the Hospitalité de Notre Dame. They usually stay in Lourdes for a period of two weeks or longer if they can afford the time.

My pilgrimages to Lourdes allowed me to draw new strength and renewed courage to help the sick in my normal every day life surrounded by sick people. Often I experienced difficulty to find the appropriate comforting words to help ease someone's pain or grief. Lourdes provided me with the experience and confidence required in these complex situations.

My professional retirement did not entail retirement from the Lourdes scene; although for some years past, I have not visited the popular town in a nursing capacity. Time spent in Lourdes as a non-working pilgrim has allowed me the opportunity to observe several alterations in the administration, policies and routine caring for the sick. Nevertheless the tender, vocational and devotional concern for the afflicted remains steadfastly unchanged.

One example of change is the participation of the sick pilgrims in the nightly torchlight procession. During my nursing days in Lourdes, this was not standard practice. Sick pilgrims did not leave the hospital after their return from the afternoon blessing of the sick. It is very gratifying to see them actively involved in this striking ceremony.

As I have said earlier, Lourdes is primarily a place for the sick, and many come to this place of hope seeking some form of cure. However, those who proclaim an inexplicable cure from their maladies are quickly and discreetly removed from the Lourdes scene.

Such people are thoroughly screened by members of the medical profession who constitute the International Commission. They are closely followed up with medical checks for the next two years after their return home. If the inexplicable cure is maintained at the end of that time, a brief notice is then published in the Lourdes press. Thus the mass hysteria which accompanied the declaration of inexplicable cures during the early days of pilgrimages to Lourdes no longer exists.

Miraculous cures are ambiguous in the sense that to establish their authenticity it would be necessary to carry out extensive clinical, chemical and scientific examinations on each person, prior to their arrival in Lourdes. If the sick person should claim that his or her ailment has suddenly left while making the pilgrimage, these examinations would have to be repeated and checked with the original results. All of this, of course, is impossible. Some neurotics state that they feel better for having visited Lourdes. This feeling may well be a psychological reaction to having spent five days in close contact with people whom they recognized as being genuinely much worse off than themselves. Neurosis and depression in their various forms are, however, grave mental disorders, which affect the physical well being of their victims. If these sufferers find relief from their afflictions through visiting the small town, who can confirm or deny that they have or have not undergone an inexplicable cure?

Nervous disorders, however, are not accepted by the Lourdes examining Medical Bureau. This is unfortunate as it suggests that each pilgrim has two separate entities: the physical and the mental, rather than being one complete person. Thousands of minor ailment sufferers may well get relief during their stay in Lourdes. Their symptomless state may be a temporary remission, or it may prove permanent. This does not prove that their symptoms would not have disappeared had they been elsewhere.

During one working holiday, I fell headlong down the hotel steps one evening. The result of my fall was a fractured right wrist. I arrived home with my arm in a plaster cast. Faith or spiritual healing can never produce any theoretical answers. It must, therefore, continue to present grave doubts and scepticism in the scientific mind. Such healing will remain shrouded in mystery until the end of time.

Chapter 9

The day-to-day routine

At five o'clock each morning the wards of the hospitals became the principal centres of activity. Patients were washed and dressed in readiness for breakfast which was served between six and half past.

Walking sick pilgrims had their meals served by the handmaids in a refectory. The more incapacitated people were fed by nurses and handmaids. As soon as the ambulant patients vacated their wards for the refectory, their beds were made, Lourdes style. This method involved drawing the bottom sheet up tightly over the pillows and tucking it under the mattress. This procedure, was probably a matter of economics, whereby expenditure on pillowcases and the laundering of them was effectively obviated. It was a routine, however, that caused considerable frustration to nurses generally. It produced frayed tempers and the occasional unladylike remark.

When toilets and treatments had been completed, the brandcardiers made their entrance with stretchers and carriages. The first loading operation of the day began as bed-bound patients were lifted from their beds and transferred to the conveyances which would transport them to morning Mass. The walking sick attended services confined to carriages, as the distance involved may well have proved too exhausting for them.

As each sick pilgrim was comfortably and securely positioned in a vehicle, he or she was moved into the foyer or courtyard where the entire contingent was aligned. (The two-wheeled carriages are black hooded single seater vehicles. A long, iron lever protruding from the centre under surface of the foot platform is the gadget by which the carriage is pulled along.) Several groups aligned at the same time. As they waited for the signal "Allez" from the French brandcardier responsible for assembling the invalids and directing them to their venues of worship, the foyer and courtyard resembled the tower of Babel. Patients and voluntary workers used that time to communicate with each other and various nationalities chattered noisily in different tongues.

As soon as the contingent received the "Allez" command, the stretcher cases were wheeled forward and the carriages fell in line behind. This 'wagon train' procession wended its way through the domain. These unique columns were guided towards different locations were Mass was being celebrated.

Some groups were directed to the grotto, others to Saint Bernadette's altar, an outdoor centre of worship, sited close to the entrance of the Rosary basilica. Several groups headed up the semicircular ramps towards the upper basilica of the Immaculate Conception.

Occasionally, a contingent was spared the effort of pulling carriages and pushing stretchers through the domain early in the morning when they were designated to the chapel inside the hospital.

Each pilgrimage group displayed its own distinctive coloured stretcher cover which corresponded to the arm bands worn by their sick pilgrims and voluntary workers. As hundreds of vividly coloured vehicles were manipulated, north, south, east and west, the domain Massabielle took on the appearance of a gigantic, mobile rainbow and was, indeed, an extremely picturesque scene.

As there was no sermon or address given during weekday Masses, the services were not prolonged. At the end of about 30 minutes, the return journey commenced. Many of the invalids preferred to remain out of doors, during the sunny mornings. For those who made such a request, their conveyances were placed underneath the tall trees at the side of the hospital.

Staff members returned to their respective hotels on a relay system, where they were served breakfast between 8.30 and 9.30. Between 10 o'clock and midday, patients were taken for pilgrimage baths, but not in such large numbers.

Situated in the grounds of the domain Massabielle, which is the focal point of all devotional services, the Asile is within easy access of all venues of worship and assembly.

Sick pilgrims and voluntary workers accommodated in the Seven Dolours Hospital are less fortunate. The location of the latter necessitates transporting invalids along part of the Rue de Grotte, then with considerable difficulty along the narrow, sloping and twisting Avenue de Bernadette Soubirous. When the narrow avenue has been negotiated it is necessary to cross a busy main thoroughfare. Saint Joseph's Gate is about 50 yards further along the boulevard. The return journey entails excessive muscle power on the part of the workers and any one who is not in the prime of health would be ill-advised to undertake this type of voluntary work.

During my voluntary nursing days, I found the

hustle and bustle associated with the serving of breakfast was repeated with the midday meal. After lunch, however, there was a lull in the activities. Some patients were taken for pilgrimage baths while the remainder enjoyed a rest until three o'clock. As far as sick pilgrims were concerned, the highlight of each day took place with their own special blessing of the sick.

Brandcardiers began loading the pilgrims into the appropriate conveyances about one hour prior to the commencement of this highly emotive ceremony which was preceded by the procession of the Blessed Sacrament. This procession began promptly at four o'clock.

It was necessary to assemble the groups in Rosarv Square some time beforehand, to enable the French brandcardiers to pack hundreds of invalid vehicles into an orderly alignment. Thanks to the dexterity of these gentlemen and others working under their direction, the vehicles were arranged in neat rows, with aisles between. The aisles were wide enough to allow the easy removal of each invalid.

There were no rules or regulations regarding groups of any nationality or special pilgrimage being placed together. The significance of the exercise was to ensure that every stricken individual was present when the blessing was administered. Where the individuals came from was of no consequence whatsoever during that ceremony.

It was during that massive gathering that the horrifying pictures illustrated in medical and nursing text books became stark realities. The hideous deformities and incurable afflictions have no special regard for sex, nationality, social status or age. Men and women from various countries, some well-dressed, some poorly clad, ranged from young babies to the aged.

The mentally incapacitated lived in a strange, illusory world. Their behaviour fluctuated between euphoria and tantrums, sometimes violence. Those caring for them could only help by conjecture, as it was impossible to understand the complexities of their troubled minds.

Physically incapacitated pilgrims, without mental impairment were trapped like animals in powerless bodies where liaison between brain centres and other organs was non-existent. Their helplessness caused total dependency on others for even the most personal and intimate bodily needs. Some suffered mental and physical afflictions.

All of them could be classified as one massive collection of catastrophic human beings who had been left behind in a rapidly progressing, scientific, medical world. All that medicine had to offer had been tried and failed. Lourdes was their last resort.

While none of them were likely to receive any visible signs of cure, they would have the consolation of knowing that they were not alone in their affliction, having met and communicated with so many others suffering the same ills and some even much worse than themselves. Because of this communication, in a great many instances, their morale had been given a terrific and well-deserved boost, leading to a sense of well-being when most of them were bereft of hope.

As the doors of the Rosary basilica opened at four o'clock, a vested priest carrying a gold jewel-studded monstrance containing the Blessed Sacrament descended the steps. He walked under a gold coloured canopy borne by four pall bearers. Following immediately behind were many more clergy, attired in cassocks, ranging in colour from the traditional black to scarlet according to status.

As they left the square after weaving in and out between the invalids, they were joined by hundreds of laity at adjacent points. Their long walk took them along the tree-lined pathways of the domain, and lasted approximately an hour and a half.

An excellent mixed voice choir, supported by music from the basilica's powerful organ and superb acoustics, sang the Latin hymns and the popular chants, 'Lauda Sion' and 'Lauda Jerusalem'. Hundreds of walkers and the less energetic hundreds who thronged the flat roofs of the basilica and crypt and the ramps leading to them, joined in the melodious form of prayer, which echoed for many miles.

Usually when the clergy re-entered the square they climbed the two flights of steps leading to the doors of the grand church. The vested priest entered in order to restore his sacred charge to the tabernacle. At this poignant stage, the invalids from each land had the comfort of hearing the blessing delivered by one of their own priests who had accompanied them to Lourdes. They heard these words:

> "You have drunk the cup of suffering which your Master drunk. You are God's chosen people.
> Oh Lord, that I may hear.
> Oh Lord, that I may see,
> Oh Lord, that I may walk. Yet not my will but thine be done."

There can be no doubt that amongst the great crowds a certain amount of scepticism prevailed. Amongst the sick pilgrims, how many possessed nagging doubts, concerning being the chosen people, when they had been so sorely stricken? Some may have wondered if their names had been erased from God's register and may well have come to regard their God as a very hard taskmaster.

To most doctors and nurses, patients are special, some perhaps a little more than others. Those patients who sat in carriages or laid on stretchers in Rosary Square were exceptionally special people to those of us who had the honour to accompany them and care for them.

All these things, of course, are not entirely without their moments of humour. Following this period of highly charged emotion, the return to normality could sometimes produce quite amusing incidents. For instance, each voluntary worker found her or himself responsible for returning the nearest invalid to the correct hospital.

British nurses often found themselves conveying non-English speaking sick pilgrims. Inability to communicate on some such occasions caused momentary spells of panic, when the worker headed in the wrong direction. A frantic display of gesticulation between patient and worker always resulted in the latter having to undertake a long haul, at a brisk pace, in order to overtake the correct line of vehicles.

On one occasion, I found myself in this position. My charge was a small, slightly built gentleman displaying a neat, goatee beard. When I turned towards him, he was signalling madly in the direction of the main gate. I realized he belonged to a pilgrimage based in the Seven Dolours Hospital.

Huge crowds of pedestrians milling around in the narrow streets made the pull upwards extremely difficult and strenuous. Bathed in perspiration, I eventually reached the summit of that steep, tortuous and constricted avenue. As I entered the courtyard of the Seven Dolours Hospital, my patient's corresponding carriage covers were already being removed.

The little man smiled and raised a thumb to indicate that all was well. No words were spoken. A big, broad shouldered brandcardier advanced towards us. As he whipped the red cover from the carriage, I noticed that the little man had no legs. As the big, grinning brandcardier was folding the waterproof cover, he inquired in a Liverpool dialect, "Where have you been, whacker? I thought you had nipped off somewhere for a pint." My legless 'foreigner' replied in an equally strong accent, "Naw, I thought I'd never see Rockferry ever again."

We all enjoyed a hearty laugh when we recovered from the surprise that we regarded each other as foreigners. Negligence on my part, in not checking the invalid's arm band was the cause of that piece of confusion which passed off very pleasantly. As I said goodbye to my little bearded friend, we agreed to look for each other in the domain during future gatherings but, as so often happens, we never did see each other again.

There was, however, an even more amusing incident to follow. As I jostled my way back through the crowded, narrow avenue, I decided to replace some of the body fluids that I had lost on the upward journey. I went into one of the cafés hoping for a cup of coffee. It seemed that almost everybody in Lourdes had the same idea at the same time.

Harassed waiters and waitresses were doing their utmost to serve impatient customers, who were placing their orders in their native tongues and expecting the overworked staff to understand. As I sipped my coffee cognac, I noticed a party of English speaking people at the adjoining table.

The party consisted of three couples, all of whom appeared to be in their late thirties or early forties. All six were grumbling furiously about being kept waiting. One of the women addressed the gentleman seated opposite to her and said, "What about all this French you know? Why can't you tell that waiter that we want some service?"

The pompous looking man sat bolt upright in his chair, adjusted his jacket with a flourish and announced to his companions, loud enough for everyone to hear, that he was going to demand service from 'yon dozey oaf'. He grabbed the tails of the jacket of the nearest waiter and said, "Gawsang. Jay fam. Fam. Voo savvy. Tray beaucoup fam." The young waiter glared at him and replied in perfect English, "Pardon Monsieur, but your wife is not my problem."

The last major event of the day to be held in the domain was the torchlight procession which took place after dark. Again the formation began in Rosary Square and on the esplanade in front of the grotto. Thousands of pilgrims queued in these two venues, often in torrential rain, as they prepared for their second long walk of the day. Each individual carried a lighted candle in a wax container. There was no musical accompaniment, but there was always a significant rendering of the entire 60 verses of the 'Ave, Ave, Ave Maria' in different languages. Each pilgrimage walked behind its own individual banner which signified the nationality of the group and where they came from. These banners are very distinctive, colourful and striking.

The procession wended its way along the pathways of the domain, then climbed the left sided ramp, leading to the upper basilica of the Immaculate Conception. They processed along the road for several yards, then returned by the ramp on the opposite side.

The massive assembly was then led in a short prayer recital by some priests within the Rosary basilica and once again the superb acoustics were employed. When the prayer recital ended, pilgrims were requested to extinguish their candles and disperse quietly. And so ended the day prayerwise. For many, it marked the beginning of a night of revelling; for others it was back to their hotels and bed.

As sick pilgrims did not participate in the torchlight procession, they were, therefore, confined to their wards after their return from their own special service. However, the fact that they had retired to bed did not mean that their day had ended. Medical inspections normally preceded the last meal of the day. It was also an appropriate period to perform treatments as they could be carried out unhurriedly. There was also some time for friendly conversation between staff and patients.

Visitors wandered around the wards like they were waiting rooms in railway or bus stations. The reason for this was that it was the only period of the day when those people could make contact with their sick relatives and friends.

As everyone concerned was on a vacation of sorts, no hard and fast rules could be laid down. Traders wheeled their large racks, displaying a wide miscellany of pious objects, from bed to bed. This exercise enabled the invalids to choose and purchase their own personal souvenirs.

Con Brannigan was always propelled on his stretcher to religious services, by one or other of the brandcardiers. It was, therefore, almost impossible for me to have any communication with him during the day. We were able to spend some time together during this rather carefree period.

Within a very short space of time, Con had become very popular with all members of our voluntary work team. Nurses, handmaids and brandcardiers flocked round his bed, exchanging pleasantries and helping him in every way possible.

His favourite person, however, was a young nun who originated from his home county in Ireland. Sister Joanne, known affectionately as Jo, was a nursing member of the Hospitalité de Notre Dame. She was not a talkative person, having rather a reticent disposition; yet she was a talented linguist and conversationalist when the occasions arose.

Jo and Con conversed about their native land. She discussed with him the art of sheep farming and its seasonal practices, such as dipping, marking and shearing. When the subject of conversation was directed to the breeding and rearing of sheep dogs, Con's face would always brighten. In his severely impaired speech, he told her many times about Ben. He always referred to Ben as 'my best auld mate' and was always careful to avoid mentioning their joint nightly escapades, concerning their visits to the Woodside Inn.

These debates took place every evening as Jo and I settled the helpless Con for the night. The exchange of views on topics which appealed to him helped to distract his attention from his doubly incontinent state, and the severity of his dreadful affliction.

Frequently he would refer to his powerless legs as 'them auld wooden planks'. Jo's jocular reply was, "Auld wooden planks, indeed. You take care of them, my lad, because I am thinking of having you signed up as a scrum half for our Lourdes rugby team."

I always related the happenings of the day, especially the amusing instances. When I told Con the story of the little gentleman with goatee beard, he laughed and replied, "But sure, Nurse, if he is a Scouser, he is a foreigner, any road."

So it was that our five days in Lourdes passed. It had been very hard work, there had been very little sleep. There had been some highly emotional moments and a great many moments of laughter, and as far as I was concerned the experience had been tremendously rewarding.

Departure day began shortly after 4 am as voluntary workers were concerned. We vacated our bedrooms in our respective hotels, transferred our luggage to bases within the hotels, then went along to our appropriate hospitals. Naturally, our patients' luggage, in some instances, had increased considerably since their arrival. As we packed their belongings, there were statuettes, figurines, musical boxes, plastic replicas complete with fairy lights of Bernadette Soubirous kneeling at the grotto, and, of course, the ubiquitous Lourdes water containers.

Instructions like 'Nurse, be careful with that' and 'mind you don't break that' and the inevitable 'Nurse, where can I put this?' would have been, in other circumstances, exasperating. This, however, was not a 'normal' situation. Despite the unearthly hour of the morning, we managed successfully to get every invalid, complete with personal paraphernalia, ready for the return journey.

Special equipment associated with nursing treatments had to be arranged in compact bundles, to allow for easy loading and unloading. Each pilgrimage had a white cabinet approximately 36 inches wide and 24 inches long. This cabinet bore a large, red cross. Inside, it had a series of small drawers and each drawer bore the name of the drug contained therein.

It was, of course, imperative that the correct medications travelled with the invalids for whom they were prescribed. As Con Brannigan belonged to that catastrophic band of people whom medicines, ancient and modern, had left behind, there was no curative pills or potions for him inside the cabinet or anywhere else.

Our homeward journey was similar to the outward one, except that I travelled in the same aircraft as Con. The entire group had, during those five days, become one great big happy family. We were all known to each other by Christian names. A most extraordinary sense of comradeship and deep friendship had developed amongst us. I felt a real twinge of sadness when the farewells began at Blackpool, as we set out on different routes to our home towns.

Father Alfred Brocklebank, in his dirty old dormobile was already there waiting. When two brandcardiers lifted Con into our parish conveyance, almost every voluntary worker came forward to say, "Ta-ra, Con. I will come and see you up yonder."

There was even more sand, more toffee papers and lollipop sticks on the floor of the dormobile. Obviously the scouts had been enjoying themselves at the seaside, while we were away. Preoccupation with my own thoughts, however, prevented me from paying much attention to the grotty interior, or to my uncomfortable position within the vehicle.

When Father Brocklebank inquired if we had enjoyed ourselves, Con assured him that everything and everybody had been wonderful. He hoped he would be able to return to Lourdes the following year. I just hoped that Con's wish would be fulfilled; for I already knew, beyond the shadow of a doubt, that I would return to nurse those sick pilgrims as often as I possibly could. There were no longer any misgivings, no mixed feelings regarding the transporting of sick people to the small French town.

Chapter 10
Life after Lourdes

To ensure that the staff of Meadowlands Hospital had not been excluded from our souvenir list and to enable Con to maintain a link with Lourdes, I had procured a rather pretty bunch of dried flowers from a vendor outside Saint Joseph's Gate. Members of the staff at Meadowlands were most appreciative and the flower arrangement was placed in a prominent position close to Con's bed.

He was accepted back into that little community with the utmost warmth and affection. Staff on duty hurried towards his bed and, with great exuberance and zeal, each one welcomed him 'home'. There were, of course, the usual quips about eating snails and frogs' legs.

A member of the domestic staff, obviously well past her prime, leaned on her polishing mop and asked, "What happened to the French man you promised to bring back for me?"

She followed her flippant inquiry by a demonstration of her personal version of the can-can, to the accompanying calls of 'Oo-la-la' from her colleagues.

It was in the midst of this warm and light-hearted sort of family gathering that Father Brocklebank and I left Con Brannigan. No doubt each of us cherished our own individual thoughts concerning the tragic individual. Both of us, however, experienced some satisfaction from the knowledge that we had played a major part in giving Con a well-deserved holiday, and had seen him returned safely and happily to the tender, loving care of the hospital staff.

On the following Sunday afternoon, I drove out to 2 Hillfoot Cottages. The resounding noise of the iron ram's head knocker was answered by Reuben, the younger member of the Brannigan family. The tall buxom 23-year-old looked at me suspiciously from underneath his bushy, sandy coloured eyebrows.

He said, "Our mam's out. She's gone t'mission hall, like."

He meant that sentence to be the end of the conversation. I intended it to be merely the beginning.

I informed Reuben in case he did not already know that his father had spent the preceding week in Lourdes. In spite of his paralysis, he had enjoyed himself immensely. He was now back in his little corner in Meadowlands. I handed Reuben a small package containing an inexpensive cross and chain and two equally inexpensive Saint Christopher medallions on chains.

Looking straight into the eyes of the young man, I continued, "Your father bought these for your mother, Alan and yourself. They are not, I am afraid, of very good quality; you see your father had very little spending money."

Reuben shifted uncomfortably in the doorway and said "Ta".

I ended our discourse by asking, "Why do you not visit your dad, Reuben? He would be so pleased to see you and Alan."

An extremely embarrassed Reuben eventually answered, "I don't have no time to go up yonder, like;

what with working all week and all, like." Still staring into his eyes, I said goodbye and left.

During the weeks immediately preceding our departure for Lourdes, I had called on Mrs Brannigan a few times and kept her up to date with the details concerning her husband. The strong brick wall which had originally existed between us, was still present, although a few dents and cracks had been achieved.

On one of these social occasions, I had accepted her offer of 'a warm drink' and joined her in a cup of tea and a delicious piece of her homemade parkin. There was still, however, a lot of work and compromise required if the brick wall was to be penetrated completely. My second visit to 2 Hillfoot Cottages in the same week was aimed at this particular objective.

If Reuben had told his mother about our confrontation on the door step, she did not mention it when I called on her a few days later. She inquired if I had enjoyed the holiday and avoided referring to her husband. When I told her how much pleasure Con had derived from his week in Lourdes, she asked, in her cynical manner, if he was still paralyzed. She sniggered and mumbled something about the whole thing being nowt but a waste of time and money. "Daft as brushes yous are, yous are that", was her assessment of those of us who had embarked on the pilgrimage.

Determined to get through to this eccentric lady and find out why she was so embittered, I let her scathing comments go unchallenged. I followed her scornful remarks with a suggestion that I call for her one afternoon each week and drive her to Meadowlands Hospital to visit her husband. I would, of course, collect her and drive her home again.

For the first time since my original meeting with Mrs Brannigan, she found herself lost for words. After she had given the matter considerable deliberation, she compromised, much to my delight. She said she was willing to accept the offer on a fortnightly basis. She went on to inquire, should she need "owt from the shops up yonder" would I wait for her. When she had been reassured that I was quite prepared to drive her to the shopping area and wait until she had made her purchases, the date was set for our first joint outing.

At first, these alternate Wednesday jaunts were difficult because of my travelling companion's virtual silence. All my attempts at small talk concerning the weather, the countryside and the poor state of the roads were met with very little response. I always drove her to the main entrance and a meeting time was arranged for our return journey. No matter how early I arrived, Mrs Brannigan was always waiting by the exit.

Usually my inquiry as to her husband's condition was answered with one word, 'champion'. When I asked if she needed anything from the shopping centre, the reply was "Nay lass, I don't want nowt." On the odd occasion when she announced that she needed "a bit of summat" from a particular store, she was driven there and I waited patiently for her to return.

Later, she developed a habit of poking her stubby forefinger at the windscreen, or the side window and sometimes twist her neck round and point at the rear window. She would, then, give me a detailed account of the financial state of "them up yonder", "them over yonder" and "them back yonder". Very few of these people were known to me, therefore their family histories, the amount of money, land and stock which they possessed were of no interest whatsoever.

On the other hand, I appreciated the fact that Mrs Brannigan's reclusive lifestyle left her with few conversational options. I adopted an attitude of listening attentively, then adding the occasional 'yes', 'no' and 'oh, really' and hoped that they had been uttered in the right places.

One very wet evening as we were making our way back to Hillfoot Cottages, Mrs Brannigan stated that one of the Turnbull's lasses was getting wed round Christmas time. Again the Turnbulls were not known to me personally. Judging by the number of milk floats that toured our locality, every morning, bearing the name 'Turnbull', it appeared that they had successfully monopolized the milk business in our entire area.

Mrs Brannigan continued, "It'll be a big do and all. She's a lucky lass. They're not without, they're not that. And she's marrying into money and land as well, she is that."

A very heavy sigh followed that little piece of information, then she continued by giving me a fairly detailed account of the prospective bridegroom's prosperity.

Six months had elapsed since Con and I had set forth on our pilgrimage to Lourdes. During those months, his little corner had become the busiest part of Meadowlands Hospital. He received lots of mail and quite a large number of diocesan pilgrimage workers visited him regularly. They brought him all sorts of presents and titbits.

Christmas preparations were very much in evidence inside the hospital, in our local shops and streets and in homes generally. However, there were no visible signs of the approaching festive season in the Brannigan's basic home. Mrs Brannigan and I were still making our regular, fortnightly excursions to and from Meadowlands Hospital.

We were always quite polite to each other, nevertheless the great barrier between us was persisting. One dismal, murky, December evening as I drove through the muddy lanes which led to Hillfoot Cottages, Mrs Brannigan leaned towards me and asked, "Would you like to see the young Turnbull lass's wedding dress?"

This was indeed a pleasant surprise, as I had never seen any of the finished articles that passed through the industrious seamstress's treadle sewing machine.

We entered the familiar cottage and Mrs Brannigan led the way up a rather dimly lit and rickety staircase. At the top of the staircase there were two bedrooms, one to the left and one to the right. She opened the door on the left and ushered me into her bright, bedroom-cum-fitting room. On a chair by the door was a neat pile of little girl's fancy and frilly dancing costumes, ready for one of our local dance teachers to collect. All around the room protective sheets were draped over finished garments which hung from the picture rail, the outside of the big, old fashioned wardrobe and the sides of the window.

Mrs Brannigan moved towards the wardrobe, lifted a hanger and removed the protective covering to reveal an exquisite traditional bridal gown of satin and lace designed in crinoline style. While I was complimenting her on her extraordinary craftsmanship, she removed some more drapes and allowed me to have a preview of the entire wedding ensemble.

Two very beautiful dresses for the bridesmaids and equally beautiful smaller versions for the flower girls. Two very attractive, little blue velvet suits for the page boys seemed to complete the consignment. As she carefully replaced the covers on the admirable array of her creations, I continued to acclaim her outstanding talents.

A very deep sigh issued forth from the industrious and gifted seamstress as she crossed the room towards the window. She removed another hanging garment which, when uncovered, displayed a most elegant and tasteful, lilac coloured dress and jacket to be worn by the bride's mother on the great day.

Mrs Brannigan replaced and re-covered that last piece of her collections. I noticed that her bottom lip was quivering and then the first tear rolled down her cheek. She took a few steps towards the big brass bed, sat heavily on the side of it. She buried her face and faded ginger head in a pillow and wept uncontrollably. I knelt on the linoleum covered floor in a gesture of sympathy. In an attempt to comfort her, I said all the things that I knew about her hard working life, the tragedy of her husband being so severely stricken. I finished by reminding her that she was fortunate in having two sons who loved her very much.

She unburied her face, sat upright, wiped her eyes and blew her nose noisily. When she had replaced her handkerchief in her cardigan sleeve, she clasped my hand tightly before disclosing her innermost secrets.

Unlike Joshua, who urged his army to blow their trumpets and raise great shouts to make the walls of

Jericho fall, the wall that separated Mrs Brannigan and myself crumbled as I listened quietly to her very unhappy life story.

Her parents and the parents of the milk magnate, George Turnbull, had more or less arranged a marriage between Hetty and George. The young couple did care for each other and most probably would have married.

Then Hetty expressed the reason for their non-union. "I started going around with yon other 'un and me mam were right when she said that I threw mesel away, for that's what I did. But you see, lass, I made mesel cheap with yon other 'un and we had to get wed. The Lord has laid his heavy hand on me ever since, he has that."

All the words of comfort and reassurance that I knew were gushing out. Thankfully, without being moralistic, patronizing or sanctimonious, I managed to help her to regain some of her composure and dignity. I surprised myself by referring to her as 'Hetty, love'.

Downstairs I made tea and while Hetty sat in one of the rocking chairs sipping from her favourite mug, I checked the hotpot in the fireside oven and set the table. When Alan and Reuben returned from work, their meal was ready and their mother was in control as always. She had deliberately and successfully cultivated a granite-like shell to conceal her broken heart and her broken life, and as far as she was concerned, Con Brannigan was entirely to blame.

Chapter 11

Con's farewell

The prospect of Con's return to Lourdes was discussed at some length by his ward sister, hospital doctor, Father Brocklebank and myself. A unanimous decision was reached that despite his gradual deterioration, he should be given the opportunity to repeat the exercise. An exercise that had brought him so much pleasure and company into his otherwise miserable existence.

The fact that this pleasure was maintained by so many members of the diocesan group and that his wife's visits had been promoted through the intervention of the group, proved very strong points in favour of his return to Lourdes. Saint Mary's Lourdes sick fund was readily available to pay our expenses.

Unlike the previous year, we became the protégés of the diocesan pilgrimage society as soon as our applications had been received by the committee members. In their usual businesslike and competent manner, they arranged every step of the journey with precision and efficiency.

Instead of the dirty dormobile, an ambulance was arranged and paid for so that Con and I could travel to and from the airport in comfort. An overnight stay in Blackpool had been obviated because of a more reasonable and convenient flight time.

A few religious services, followed by feasting in an adjoining hall, had been held in the Preston area during the previous year. These meetings had helped to keep voluntary workers in contact with each other. When our reunion inside the small terminal took place, the majority of us treated the occasion as another friendly get-together. There were a few new faces among those of us who set about the task of assembling another contingent of sick pilgrims. Searching their various items of luggage, in a bid to retrieve passports from their 'safe places', had become a necessary and customary part of the procedure.

Inquiries concerning some of our last year's sick pilgrims revealed that quite a few of them had died. It was not surprising to learn that the handsome leukaemia sufferer was among the deceased. I was, however, quite saddened to learn that my health visitor, paraplegic friend had also passed away.

Con was the only sick pilgrim present who had travelled with us on a previous pilgrimage. As usual, he was being treated like royalty, with nurses, handmaids and brandcardiers greeting him enthusiastically. There was only one other stretcher case, a middle-aged lady who was suffering from advanced kidney failure.

When the entire sick contingent was aligned, we moved towards the passport control desk, then a few yards further along to the flight desk, through the flight gates towards the waiting planes. Unlike the previous year, I found myself totally responsible for Con Brannigan. The routine loading of the plane was completed without any hitches. And so, yet another group of people, unfortunate enough to be left behind by the rapidly advancing, scientific world of medicine, was on the last sojourn of hope to the city of the sick in the foothills of the Pyrenees.

Lunch was served aboard the plane and the familiar feeding of patients commenced. Con, despite his severe paralysis, could swallow quite well. Apart from the occasional bout of regurgitation, meal times presented no problem. When his meal was finished, I assisted a young blind man to remove the polythene covering from his food in the plastic container. My further offer of help was refused by his blunt assertion that he was quite capable of taking care of himself. Later, I learned that this unfortunate 23-year-old ex-soldier had been blinded by a bomb explosion in Northern Ireland. He was an angry and resentful young man and who could blame him?

Without incident we arrived at Tarbes where the officials boarded the plane and checked the passports. As they left, the cheerful French brandcardiers with their native greeting, 'Soyez les bienvenus', arrived and helped to unload our incapacitated travellers. Within a very short space of time, we were safely ensconced inside our converted coach en route for Lourdes.

Our driver, thankfully, was considerably more cautious and considerate than our previous one had been. My colleague and I were able to supervise our two stretcher cases without difficulty. As the coach weaved its way through the narrow, tortuous and souvenir cluttered streets, I clutched Con's hand and said, "We are back in Lourdes, Con."

His face lit up, his squinted eyes stared in the direction of the ceiling and he said quietly and distinctly, "Thank God. I want to stay here."

Apart from being allocated to a different ward in the Asile, everything was fairly similar to the previous visit, except that Jo was absent. I knew by the number of times that Con mentioned her name that he was missing her very much.

Routines remain unchanged, the very early start to each day, the frustrating bedmaking procedure, morning Mass with the colourful wagon train traversing the domain, stints of duty in the bathing area and the highlight of each day, the blessing of the sick, were very much a repetition of our earlier pilgrimage. At the end of five days, the very early morning packing ritual was repeated, in preparation for our return to England.

On the last day of our stay in Lourdes, the doctor in charge of the pilgrimage considered Con unfit to attend the blessing of the sick ceremony, because of his recently developed chest infection. Although it was evident that he was breathing with great difficulty, the medical order upset both Con and myself.

A course of antibiotics was commenced in the hope that his infection would ease sufficiently to allow us to travel home. Con kept repeating, "I'm not all that bothered about going back, any road. I'd rather stay where I'm at."

He was certified medically fit to travel. In spite of a harsh spasmodic cough and some breathlessness, we did manage, by treating him like a piece of Dresden china, to get him back to the warmth and friendliness of Meadowlands Hospital.

As soon as he was received into his little corner and I was in possession of my car, I went immediately to Hetty and informed her of Con's poorly condition. She did not suggest that she should visit him. After some persuasion over our customary cup of tea, she decided that she would 'go up yonder' on Wednesday. I pointed out that today was only Friday. He was desperately ill and might die before

Wednesday. Hetty flatly refused to alter her visiting schedule.

Con recovered from his chest infection. However, they became recurrent and more frequent. Each attack left him weaker and more helpless. His loyal friends continued to travel from all parts of the diocese to call on him. Hetty gave him half an hour of her time once a fortnight and I called on him two or three times a week.

His son, Alan, began visiting his father fairly regularly. This change of heart was brought about through the influence of his girlfriend, Eunice, who later became his wife. Eunice's mother suffered from rheumatoid arthritis. She was admitted to Meadowlands Hospital periodically for a few weeks, in order that Eunice and her father could have a rest. Alan accompanied his girlfriend when she visited her mother. Eunice, who was a very caring young lady, insisted that they went along to see Con. When her mother was discharged from hospital, she continued to visit her future father-in-law and managed, successfully, to make Alan aware of his filial duties.

Reuben appeared once at his father's bedside and said, "Our mam's got the 'flu, so give us the sick note, will ya. So as she can get the money, like."

When he had picked up the signed insurance certificate from the locker drawer, he said, "Ta-ra", and left.

Christmas came and went with the usual rushing, crushing and spending. The joint fortnightly drives between Hillfoot Cottages and Meadowlands Hospital continued, and Hetty's little offerings of tea and cakes and often a freshly baked loaf to take home had become normal practice. And so the weeks and months went past. Soon the Lourdes pilgrimage was fast approaching once again.

The general consensus of opinion of those of us immediately concerned with Con, was that he was, most certainly, unfit to travel. He was, however, becoming increasingly upset about this joint decision reached by the hospital doctor, the ward sister, Father Brocklebank and myself. Father Brocklebank discussed the subject with Con and explained that there was a strong possibility that he would not survive the journey.

Con beamed and set his squinted eyes on the face of the chaplain and said, "But sure I don't want to come back, any road. I didn't want to come back last time."

That was the little speech that changed all our minds. As the silvery haired doctor completed the now familiar application form, he raised his head, smiled at the ward sister and myself and said, "It must be nice to have faith like Mr Brannigan's."

The subject of this particular forthcoming pilgrimage was going to be an extremely important part of my next heart to heart talk with Hetty. She was no longer scathing about Lourdes when the subject arose. She still remained apathetic when Con's name entered into the conversation. This apathy and phlegmatic attitude extended to the subject of his death, as I was to discover during our tea drinking sessions.

When I questioned Hetty about her wishes concerning the possibility of his dying in Lourdes, she replied, "He keeps on telling me when I am up yonder seeing him that he wants to stay over yonder. Happen it would be the best thing all round. Let him stay over yonder, then, and let that be an end to it for good and all."

Con improved considerably when he learned that his third trip to Lourdes had been authorized. Although his condition had deteriorated somewhat during the past 12 months, he was quite bright and doing his best to regain his former jocularity. For almost six weeks prior to our departure date, his chest remained reasonably clear of infection.

However, once again, I set off for Lourdes with very mixed feelings. One of the ambulance drivers, on the way to the airport, passed a remark which stayed with me all the way. He was gazing down at the sleeping Con in the back of the vehicle when he said, "You have taken on something there, my lass. He looks very dodgy to me."

All the way across in the plane and during the next few days that comment resounded through my brain. Each time I looked at Con's twisted body lying awkwardly in bed in one of the single rooms in the Asile, I could only agree wholeheartedly with the driver's observation.

On our first day in Lourdes, Con was prohibited from attending services, as our pilgrimage doctor felt that he was exhausted following the journey. He was, however, allowed to attend the blessing of the sick the following day. An added bonus appeared on our second day in the form of Jo, who had returned for a further period of duty on behalf of the Hospitalité de Notre Dame. There was always a few unfit patients left inside the hospital during religious services, therefore a few members of staff were detailed to look after them.

It was during the procession of the Blessed Sacrament on the afternoon of our third day in Lourdes. As I stood in Rosary Square in the midst of the familiar stretchers and invalid carriages my mind was in a turmoil because of Con's poor condition.

During the night he had developed another one of his respiratory infections. Fortunately, Jo was on hospital duty; I held high hopes of her getting him through this latest setback. As the clergy were re-entering the square, I felt the tap on my shoulder and one of the brandcardiers beckoned me out of the crowd. He merely said,

"Sorry, luv, he has just gone about 15 minutes ago."

The rigorous training involved in preparation for the religious life, seems on the surface, to deprive nuns of any demonstrative signs of emotion. The dark brown foyer of the Asile seemed more formidable than ever, as I made my way to the single room at the far end of the long ward. Jo was already sorting out Con's few personal belongings.

As I gently lifted the sheet that covered his face, he seemed to be wearing his big, beaming smile. I could almost hear the slurred words, "I want to stay there, any road." As the tears spilled down my face, a thoroughly composed Sister Joanne rebuked me. She told me that I was being sorry for myself instead of being thankful that Con's prayer had been answered and for the privilege of having accompanied him to Lourdes on three occasions.

I hesitated at the door of the small room on my way out. I explained to the very serene lady that Con had been doubly privileged. Firstly, his prayer to die in Lourdes had been answered. Secondly, his departure from this world had taken place in the company of someone from his native land, some one whom he held in high esteem.

I concluded by saying, "Thanks Jo for everything and especially for being here today."

Funeral arrangements were conducted by telephone between our chaplain to the sick pilgrims and Father Brocklebank. When the latter telephoned my hotel later that evening, he informed me that he had gone immediately to 2 Hillfoot Cottages after receiving the original message confirming Con's death.

He had tried to persuade Hetty to accompany him to Saint Mary's presbytery where she could speak on the telephone to the Lourdes chaplain. She had, of course, flatly refused. He did, however, manage to obtain her written signature authorizing her husband's funeral to take place in Lourdes. Con's funeral was arranged for 10 o'clock in the morning of our departure

Our farewell tribute to Con would most certainly have been described by his widow as 'a big do'. On the evening prior to his internment, his remains were received into the parish church in Peyramale Square, with a moving and prayerful ceremony. An overnight vigil of at least six people at the same time was maintained. The vigil was maintained by our own group members and a number local people also stayed overnight as a mark of respect towards the visitor who had died in their town.

The following morning Requiem Mass was concelebrated by several priests belonging to our pilgrimage after which the cortege left, in torrential rain, for the local cemetery. The black hearse wended its way through narrow streets, across the bridge, along the main thoroughfare towards Lourdes burial ground.

The cortege consisted of every member of our group. Members of the Hospitalité de Notre Dame had kindly offered to look after our already packed, ready to move, patients for us during the funeral period. There were a great many members of other groups who joined our procession as a token of comradeship. Quite a number of us carried small floral arrangements, as our last gifts to a much loved friend.

Local inhabitants involved in their daily routines, stopped on the pavements. The men removed their berets and joined with the women in crossing themselves as we went past. Our chaplain to the sick recited the liturgical, graveside prayers, then led us in the singing the very beautiful 'Salve Regina'.

It was thus, on "a mucky auld mornin" that Cornelius Brendan Aloysius Brannigan, the 51-year-old Irish shepherd, who had spent most of his life on the lonely, windswept Cumbrian fells, was laid to rest. His resting place is situated in the shadows of the sheep folds where Bernadette Soubirous, the 14-year-old shepherdess tended her flocks so many years before.

Ten years and as many Lourdes pilgrimages later, I stood in the fitting room-cum-bedroom in 2 Hillfoot Cottages. I was being fitted with my new winter coat. Hetty Brannigan moved on her knees round my ankles, busily engaged in pinning up the hem of the unfinished garment.

With her mouth full of pins she said, "All them times you've been over yonder, happen, mebbe you've seen some miracles. Have you?"

I stared at the little window with green cotton curtains, a replica of the ones downstairs. It was underneath the window downstairs where the uncomfortable camp bed had been positioned and on which Con had spent the early days of his affliction. Those early days had been so very difficult for all of us, especially for Con and his increasingly malfunctioning body.

Hetty had, for many years, practised the art of concealing her emotions. She sheltered in her granite-like shell. Yet it must have been quite a traumatic experience for her to learn that her very active husband was suffering from a progressive paralyzing disease.

Memories of erstwhile experiences must have overwhelmed me. When Hetty repeated her query, I had to jolt myself into the present. Still gazing at the green cotton curtains, I answered her question concerning miracles with, "Yes, Hetty, I have actually witnessed a miracle associated with Lourdes. It happened quite a long time ago".